The Young Colonists ... New edition.

G. A. Henty

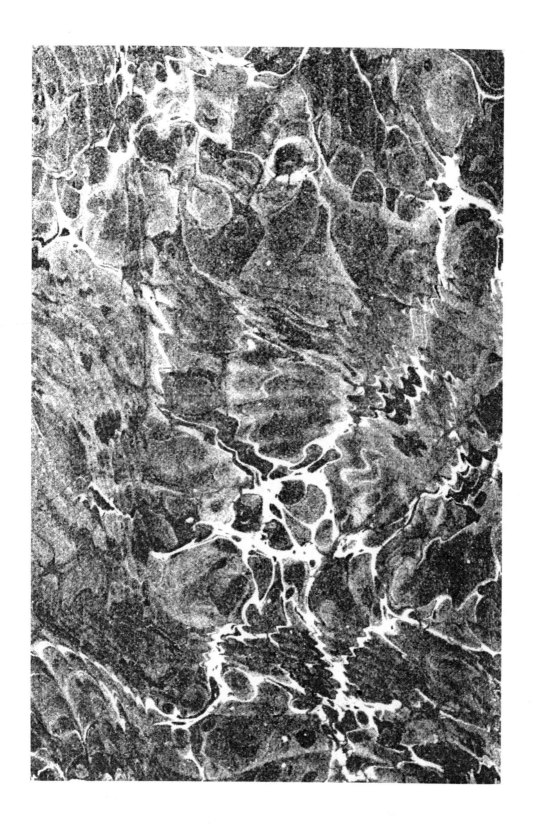

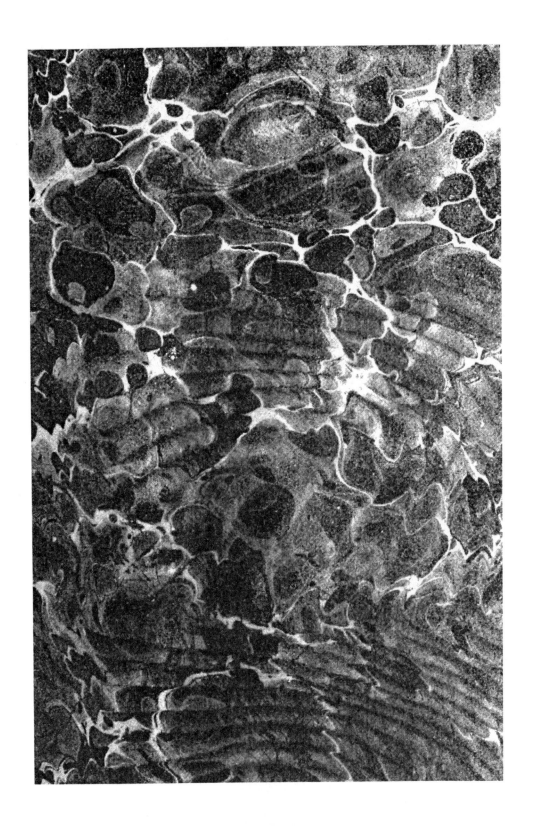

"TOM FIRED INTO THE THICK OF THE DEER AND
ONE OF THEM FELL."

THE YOUNG COLONISTS

A STORY OF

THE ZULU AND BOER WARS

BY

G. A. HENTY

Author of "With Clive in India", "The Cat of Bubastes", "In the Reign of Terror",
"In Freedom's Cause", "By England's Aid", "By Pike and Dyke", "Held Fast for England"
&c. &c.

WITH SIX ILLUSTRATIONS BY SIMON H. VEDDER

NEW EDITION

GLASGOW:
BLACKIE & SON, LIMITED.

TORONTO:

WILLIAM BRIGGS, 29-33 RICHMOND ST. WEST.
THE COPP, CLARK COMPANY, LIMITED, 9 FRONT ST. WEST.

PREFACE.

As a rule the minor wars in which this country has been from time to time engaged, have been remarkable both for the admirable way in which they were conducted and for the success that attended them. The two campaigns in South Africa, however, that followed each other with but a brief interval, were notable exceptions. In the Zulu War the blunder, made by the General in command, of dividing his army and marching away with the greater portion without troubling himself to keep up communication with the force left behind, brought about a serious disaster at Isandula. In the Boer War we also suffered two defeats,—one at Laing's Neck, the other at Majuba Hill,—and when at last a British force was assembled capable of retrieving these misfortunes, the English government decided not to fight, but to leave the Boers in possession of the Transvaal. This unfortunate surrender has, assuredly, brought about the troubled state of things now existing in South Africa.

After having written upwards of fifty records of almost unbroken success to the British arms in almost all parts of the world, I have found it painful to describe these two campaigns in which we suffered defeat. I trust, however, that this story will prove of great interest to the reader because of the characteristic English pluck and daring of its hero

G. A. HENTY.

CONTENTS.

ILLUSTRATIONS.

THE YOUNG COLONISTS.

CHAPTER I.

A SNOW-DRIFT.

THE country round Castleton, in Derbyshire, is greatly admired by summer tourists, for it lies in the wildest part of that county; but in winter the wind whistles sharply over the bleak hills—where there are no trees to break its violence,—the sheep huddle under the shelter of the roughly-built stone walls, and even lovers of the picturesque would at that season prefer a more level and wooded country. The farm of Mr. Humphreys was situated about a mile from Castleton. It consisted of 100 acres or so of good land in the bottom, and of five or six times as much upland grazing on the hills. Mr. Humphreys owned as well as farmed his land, and so might have claimed, had he chosen, the title of gentleman-farmer ; but he himself would have scoffed at such an idea. He was a hard-working, practical farmer, about over his ground from morning to night, save when the hounds met within easy distance in winter ; then he would mount "Robin," who served alike as hunter, or hack.

or to drive in the neat dog-cart to Buxton market; and, although there were many handsomer horses in the field, Mr. Humphreys was seldom far off when the fox was killed.

His family consisted of his wife and two sons, the eldest, Richard, was about fourteen years old. His brother, John, was three years younger. Both went to school at Castleton. The younger boy was fond of his books; he had always been weak and delicate, and, being unable to spend his time in active exercise out of doors, he was generally to be found reading by the fire in winter, or lying on the ground in summer under a tree in the orchard, with his chin on his hand, and the book before him. Richard had no literary taste; he managed to scrape through his work and keep a moderate place in his class, somewhere about half-way down; but he threw his whole heart into outdoor exercise, and was one of the best bats in the school, although there were many there older by years. He knew every foot of the hills, could tell every bird by its note, and knew all about their nests and eggs. Except in school, or perhaps during the long winter evenings, it was rare indeed to find Dick with a book in his hand.

" You will never set the Thames on fire, Dick," his father would say to him.

"I shall never want to, father," he would reply. "I do not see that learning will ever be much good to me."

"That is a foolish idea, Dick. A great deal of the learning that boys get at school is of no actual value in pounds, shillings, and pence. It is not the fact of knowing Latin, and Greek, and mathematics which benefits a man; but it is the learning of them. It is the discipline to the mind, which is of benefit. The mind is like the body. There is no use in cricket, or in boating, or in hunting, but these things strengthen the body and make it active and healthy, and able to do better everything which it undertakes, and it is exactly the same thing with the mind; besides, the days are coming when farmers must farm their land with science and intelligence, or they will be left behind in the race. We are being rivalled by the farmers of America. Not only do we have to pay rent, but by the tithes and rates and taxes they put upon us government makes the English farmer pay a heavy tax upon every bushel of corn he produces, while they allow the American corn to come into the market tax-free. This may be all right, but it does not appear fair to me. However, there it is, and we have got to meet it, and if we are to keep our heads above water, it can only be by farming up to the very best lights of the day."

"Well, father," Dick said, "then it seems to me that when we grow up, John and I must farm together. He shall be the scientific partner; I will do the work."

"That is all right enough, Dick, but you must

have some science too, else you and he will never get on. You would want to go on in the old-fashioned groove, and would call his ideas new-fangled. No, I intend you, when you get old enough, to go to Cirencester College, where you will learn the theory and science of farming thoroughly. You will get the practical part at home. As to John, he is a child yet, and, I trust, will grow up strong and active ; but if his tastes remain as they now are, I do not think it likely he will take to farming, and we must find some other career for him."

One afternoon in the beginning of December two of Dick's school-fellows said to him,—

"We are going over the hills to our uncle's farm, Dick. Will you go with us ? "

When there was nothing better to do, Dick was always ready for a walk, and he at once agreed to accompany the Jacksons. The elder boy was about his own age, the younger two years his junior.

The Jacksons called for him directly he had finished his dinner, and they started away together for a farm which was about four miles distant. They struck right across the hills, as it would have been two miles longer by the nearest road.

"I should not be surprised," Dick said, "if it were to snow to-night; it is bitterly cold, and the clouds look very heavy."

"I hope it won't snow until we get back," James, the younger of the brothers, remarked.

"I don't know," Dick answered, looking at the clouds. "I should not be surprised if it began at any moment."

The wind was blowing strongly. The hills were high and steep, and, although the boys made their best speed, it was considerably over an hour before they reached the farm. They had started at two, and it was now a quarter past three. Mr. Jackson was out. The boys delivered the message with which they had been charged to their aunt.

"Now," she said, "I will cut you each a hunch of cake, and when you have eaten that and had a glass of fresh milk you had best start at once. It is bitterly cold, and we are going to have snow. The sooner you are home, the better."

The boys now ate their cake. Mrs. Jackson came to the door with them. Then she said, as the first flake of snow fell,—

"I am not sure, boys, that you had not better stay here all night."

The boys laughed.

"Why, what would they say at home? They would just be in a way about us."

"Well, at any rate, you had better go by the road."

"Oh, that is two miles farther at least. We should not get home until long after dark. We shan't be an hour by the hills. We know every foot of the way."

"Well, good-bye, then. Make as much haste as you can."

For half a mile their way led along the road, then they scrambled over a wall and began to ascend the barren hill-side. The snow was falling fast now. Thicker and thicker it came down, and when, hot and panting, they reached the top of the hill, the wind blew the flakes so fiercely into their faces that they were half-blinded, and were obliged to turn their backs to the gale while they got breath. For half an hour they struggled on. They could scarcely see ten paces before them through the driving snow, and in every sheltered spot white patches rapidly began to form.

"How different things look in a snow-storm!" Dick said, as they stopped for breath and shelter under the lee of a wall. "I don't know, Tom, but I am not quite sure that we are going straight; I do not know what wall this is."

"No more do I," Tom Jackson replied. "I felt quite sure that we were going right at first, but somehow I don't think so now."

"I wish the snow would stop for a minute," Dick said, "just to let us have a look round. If I could see a hundred yards I am sure I should know where we are. What is the matter with you, James; what are you blubbering about?"

"My feet are so cold ; they hurt dreadfully."

"Oh, never mind," Dick said. "Come, boys, push along, and we shall soon be home."

Again they started with heads bent to face the storm.

"It is getting dark awfully fast," Tom Jackson said.

"It is, and no mistake. Come, let us have a trot. Come on, young one."

But, although Dick spoke hopefully, he was not as confident as he appeared. He was sure now that they had lost the way. They might not, he hoped, be far off the track ; but he knew that they were not following the precise line by which they came.

It was now nearly dark. The snow was falling thicker than ever, and the ground, except upon the uplands exposed to the full force of the wind, was covered with a white mantle.

On arriving at the bottom of a steep hill, they stopped again.

"Do you know where we are, Tom ?"

"Not in the least," Tom answered.

"This ought to be the last valley," Dick said, " and after one more climb we ought to go straight down into Castleton. Don't you remember in that valley there were a lot of sheep in a fold, with a wall round it ? If we can find that, we shall know that we are right. It is near the bottom, so we shall not miss it. Which way shall we turn, left or right ?"

"Let us try the left first," Tom said.

They walked for half a mile, gradually ascending.

"It is not this way," Tom said at last. "We are getting to the head of the valley. What are you doing, James?" as the young boy, who had been sobbing for some time, threw himself on the snow.

"I cannot go any farther," he murmured. "I am so cold, and so tired, and so sleepy."

"Oh, nonsense!" Dick said. "Here, take hold of his arm, Tom, and lift him up; give him a good shake; he must go on; he would die if he stopped here."

The two lads raised the younger boy, and half-supporting half-dragging him turned and retraced their footsteps.

It was pitch dark now, and they could not see a yard before them. For some time they continued their way.

"There is no shepherd's hut. Certainly, this is not the valley. What on earth are we to do?"

"I don't know," Tom said, beginning to cry.

"Shut up, Tom Jackson. What are you thinking about? This is no time for howling like a baby; you have got to think of what is best to do. It is no use climbing the next hill, for we might be going away from home, instead of getting nearer. Besides, we should have to haul Jimmy up, for he can scarcely stand now; and, although it is bitterly cold here, it would be worse on the top of the hill. No, we have got to stop here all night, that is clear."

"We shall be dead before morning!" Tom roared.

"I will hit you in the eye, Tom Jackson, if you don't shut up; you are as bad as a girl; I am ashamed of you. Now, what we have got to do, is to find some sort of shelter, either a wall or bush, and we must keep on until we come to something. Keep awake, Jimmy; we shan't have much farther to go, and then you can lie down quietly."

They went on for a bit.

"It is no use," Dick said. "They don't put walls across bottoms; more likely to find one either to the right or left. Now, Tom, you stop here for a minute or two, and I will look about; you keep shouting every minute, so that I can find my way back to you."

Turning off, he began to ascend the next hill, and in two or three minutes shouted the glad news to Tom that he had found the wall; then he returned.

Jimmy, cheered at the prospect of lying down, made an effort, and they soon reached the wall.

Like most of the walls in Derbyshire, it was formed of flat stones laid without mortar, some four feet high.

"Now, Tom, set to work; get some stones off the wall on both sides, and build up two other walls against this; three feet wide inside will do, and just long enough to lie in. Here, Jimmy, you help; it will keep you awake, and, you see, the higher we make the walls the snugger it will be; we will have quite a nice house."

The boys all set to work, and in half an hour three walls were built. At the point where the two side walls touched the other, they were three feet high, and sloped down to two at the lower end.

"Now, Jimmy, you chuck the snow out. Tom and I will go, one each way, along the wall; likely enough we may come upon some bushes—they often grow in shelter of the walls: if we can find a few sticks we will cover the house over. Lots of these stones are a couple of feet long, and we will manage a sort of roof. The snow will soon cover it, and we shall be as warm as possible."

A quarter of an hour later the two boys returned; both had been successful and brought a bundle of sticks; these were laid across the top, interspersed with smaller twigs, the ends being kept down with stones to prevent their being blown away. The last were placed in position after the boys had crept inside. They did not attempt to roof it with stones, for the supply of sticks and brushwood was large enough to catch the snow-flakes as they fell, and these would soon form a covering, while it would have been difficult to balance the stones.

Jimmy was by this time in a state almost of lethargy; but the others were fairly warm from their exertions. They now lay down close beside the younger boy, one on each side. At first they felt the cold extremely.

"Let us keep awake as long as we can," Dick said.

"I don't feel inclined to sleep at all," Tom answered; "my hands and feet feel frozen, but I am warm enough everywhere else, and the ground is precious hard and bumpy."

"I am only afraid about Jimmy," Dick said; "he is sound asleep, and he was so awfully cold; lie as close as you can to him, Tom, and put your arm over him and keep your legs huddled up against his."

"It feels warmer than it did," he went on, after a pause of half an hour; "don't you think so, Tom?"

"A lot warmer," Tom said. "I expect the snow has made a good thick roof."

"Yes, and the wind does not blow through the stones as it did. I expect the snow is drifting up all round; it was getting very deep against the wall when we got in, and if it goes on all night, Tom, I should not wonder if we are covered deep before morning. The wind always sweeps it off the hills, and makes deep drifts in the bottoms."

"What shall we do, then?"

"I don't know," Dick answered; "but there will be plenty of time to think of that in the morning. I think Jimmy is all right, Tom; I have just put my hand inside his waistcoat and he feels quite warm now. Say your prayers, and then let us try to get off to sleep."

This they were not very long in doing, for the air in the little hut was soon heated by the action of their bodies. Outside the storm was still raging, and the wind, laden with swirling snow from the uplands, was piling it high in the valleys. Already the hut was covered and the wall behind it.

All night and all next day the snow continued to fall; the next day, and the next, it kept on. Old folks down in Castleton said they never remembered such a storm. It lay three feet deep in the fields, and there was no saying how deep the drifts might be in the hollows. For the first two days the wind had tried its best to keep the hills clear, but it had tired of the work, and for the last two had ceased to blow, and the great feathered flakes formed steadily and silently.

Tom was the first to wake.

"Holloa!" he exclaimed, "where are we? Oh! I remember. Dick, are you awake?"

"Yes, I am awake now," Dick said. "What is it? It is not morning yet. I seem to have been asleep a long time, and don't my bones just ache? Jimmy, old boy, are you all right?"

"Yes," Jimmy grunted.

"It is quite warm," Dick said. "It feels very close, and how still it is! The wind has quite gone down. Do you know, Tom, I think it must be morning. There seems a faint sort of light. I can see the stones in the wall behind you."

"So it must," Tom assented. "Oh! how stifling it is!" and he raised himself into a sitting position.

"I am afraid we are buried deep in the snowdrift. Put your hand up, Tom ; don't you feel some of these sticks are bent in the middle?"

"Ever so much; there must be a great weight on them. What are we to do, Dick; shall we try and dig a way out?"

"That will be no good," Dick answered; "not if it is deep; and if it has been snowing all night, there is no saying how deep it may be this morning down in this bottom. This drift-snow is like dust. I remember last winter that Bill Jones and Harry Austin and I tried to make a tunnel in a deep drift, but the snow fell in as fast as we scraped it away. It was just like dry sand."

"We are all right for warmth," Tom said; "but it feels quite stifling."

"Yes, we must try and get some air," Dick said. "The roof-sticks are close together down at our feet. There were three or four left over when we had finished, so we can take them away without weakening the roof. We might shove one of them up through the snow."

The sticks were removed carefully, but a quantity of fine snow fell in on their feet. One was then shoved up through the top, but the only effect, when it was removed, was that it was followed by some snow powdering down on their faces.

"Let us tie four of them together," Dick said. "I have plenty of string in my pocket."

This was done, fresh sticks being tied to the bottom as the first were shoved up through the snow.

"Now, Tom, help me to work it about a bit, so as to press the snow all round, and make a sort of tube."

For some time a shower of little particles fell as they worked, but gradually these ceased. Then the stick was cautiously lowered, being untied joint by joint, and looking up the boys gave a shout of pleasure. At the top of the hole, which was some six inches wide at the bottom, was a tiny patch of light.

"We have only just reached the top," Dick said; "the snow must be near fifteen feet deep."

Small though the aperture was, it effected a sensible relief. The feeling of oppression ceased; half an hour later the hole was closed up, and they knew that the snow was still falling.

Another length of stick was added, and the daylight again appeared.

The boys slept a good deal; they had no sensation of cold whatever, the heat of their bodies keeping the air at a comfortable temperature. They did not feel so hungry as they expected, but they were very thirsty.

"I shall eat some snow," Tom said.

"I have heard that that makes you more thirsty," Dick remarked; "hold some in your hands till it melts, and then sip the water."

Four days passed; then they found that the snow no longer continued to cover up the hole, and knew that the snow-storm had ceased. The number of sticks required to reach the top was six, and as each of these was about four feet long they knew that, making allowance for the joints, the snow was over twenty feet deep.

Very often the boys talked of home, and wondered what their friends were doing. The first night, when they did not return, it would be hoped that they had stayed at the farm; but somebody would be sure to go over in the morning to see, and when the news arrived that they were missing, there would be a general turn out to find them.

" They must have given up all hope by this time,"
Dick said, on the fifth morning, " and must be pretty
sure that we are buried in the drift somewhere ; but,
as all the bottoms will be like this, they will have
given up all hopes of finding our bodies till the thaw
comes."

" That may be weeks," Tom said ; " we might as
well have died at once."

" We can live a long time here," Dick replied confidently. " I remember reading once of a woman
who had been buried in the snow being got out
alive a tremendous time afterwards. I think it was
five weeks, but it might have been more. Hurrah !
I have got an idea, Tom."

" What is that ?" Tom asked.

" Look here ; we will tie three more sticks—"

" We can't spare any more sticks," Tom said ;
" the snow is up to our knees already."

" Ah ! but thin sticks will do for this," Dick
said ; " we can get some thin sticks out here. We
will tie them over the others, and on the top of all
we will fasten my red pocket-handkerchief, like a
flag ; if any one comes down into this bottom they
are sure to see it."

CHAPTER II.

THE RED FLAG.

DICK'S plan was soon carried into effect, and the little red flag flew as an appeal for help ten feet above the snow in the lonely valley.

Down in Castleton events had turned out just as the boys had anticipated. The night of the snow-storm there was no sleep for their parents, and at daybreak, next morning, Mr. Humphreys and Mr. Jackson set out on foot through the storm for the distant farm. They kept to the road, but it took them four hours to reach the farm, for the drifts were many feet deep in the hollows, and they had the greatest difficulty in making their way through.

When, upon their arrival, they found the boys had left before the gale began, their consternation and grief were extreme, and they started at once on their return to Castleton.

Search-parties were immediately organized, and these, in spite of the fury of the storm, searched the hills in all directions.

After the first day, when it was found that they were not at any of the shepherds' huts scattered among the hills, all hopes of finding them alive ceased. So hopeless was it considered, that few parties went out on the three following days; but on the fifth, when the snow-storm ceased and the sun shone out, numbers of men again tramped the hills in the vague hope of finding some sign of the missing boys; they returned disheartened. The snow was two feet deep everywhere, twenty in many of the hollows.

The next day but few went out, for the general feeling was, that the bodies could not be discovered until the thaw came, and at present it was freezing sharply.

Among those who still kept up the search were several of the boys' school-fellows. They had not been permitted to join while the snow-storm continued, and were therefore fresh at the work. A party of four kept together, struggling through the deep snow-drifts, climbing up the hills, and enjoying the fun, in spite of the saddening nature of their errand.

On arriving at the brow of a deep valley five miles from home, they agreed that they would go no farther, as it was not likely that the missing boys could have wandered so far from their track. That they had in fact done so was due to a sudden change in the direction of the wind; it had been driving in their faces when they started, and with bent down heads they had struggled against it, unconscious that it was sharply changing its direction.

"Just let us have a look down into the bottom," one of the boys said; "there may be a shepherd's hut here."

Nothing, however, was seen, save a smooth, white surface of snow.

"What is that?" one exclaimed suddenly. "Look, there is a little red flag flying down there—come along."

The boys rushed down the hill at full speed.

"Don't all go near the flag," one said; "you may be treading on their bodies."

They arrived within ten yards of the flag, in which they soon recognized a red pocket-handkerchief. They were silent now, awe-struck at the thought that their companions were lying dead beneath.

"Perhaps it is not theirs," the eldest of the party said presently. "Anyhow I had better take it off and carry it home."

Treading cautiously and with a white face, for he feared to feel beneath his feet one of the bodies of his friends, he stepped, knee-deep in the snow-drift, to the flag. He took the little stick in his hand to pluck it up; he raised it a foot, and then gave a cry of astonishment and started back.

"What is the matter?" the others asked.

"It was pulled down again," he said in awe-struck tones. "I will swear it was pulled down again."

"Oh, nonsense!" one of the others said; "you are dreaming."

"I am not," the first replied positively; "it was regularly jerked in my hand."

"Can they be alive down there?" one suggested.

"Alive! How can they be alive after five days, twenty feet deep in the snow? Look at the flag!"

There was no mistake this time; the flag was raised and lowered five or six times. The boys took to their heels and ran and gathered in a cluster fifty yards away on the hillside.

"What can it be?" they asked, looking in each others' pale faces.

The behaviour of the flag seemed to them something supernatural.

"We had better go back and tell them at home," one of them said.

"We can't do that; no one would believe us. Look here, you fellows," and he glanced round at the bright sky, "this is nonsense; the flag could not wave of itself; there must be somebody alive below; perhaps there is a shepherd's hut quite covered with the drift, and they have pushed the flag up through the chimney."

The supposition seemed a reasonable one, and a little ashamed of their panic the group returned towards the flag. The eldest boy again approached it.

"Go carefully, Tomkins, or you may fall right down a chimney."

The flag was still continuing its up and down movement; the boy approached and lay down on the snow close to it; then he took hold of the stick; he felt a pull, but held fast; then he put his mouth close to the hole, two or three inches in diameter, through which it passed.

"Halloa!" he shouted; "is any one below?"

A cry of "Yes, yes," came back in reply. "The two Jacksons and Humphreys."

"Hurrah!" he shouted at the top of his voice, and his companions, although they had not heard the answer, joined in the cheer.

"Are you all right?" he shouted down again.

"Yes, but please get help and dig us out."

"All right; I will run all the way back; they will have men here in no time; good-bye; keep up your spirits."

"They are all there below!" he shouted to his friends. "Come on, you fellows, there is not a moment to lose."

Wild with excitement the boys made their way home; they rushed down the hill-sides, scrambled through the drifts in the bottoms, in which they sometimes disappeared altogether, and had to haul each other out, struggled up the hills, and, panting and breathless, rushed in a body into Mr. Humphreys' farmhouse, that standing nearest to them, on their way to Castleton.

"We have found them; we have found them," they panted out. "They are all alive."

Mrs. Humphreys had risen from her seat in a chair by the fire as the boys entered, and uttering a faint cry fell back insensible.

At this moment the farmer, who had but five minutes before returned, having been out since daybreak on the hills, hurried into the room; he was taking off his heavy boots when he heard the rush of feet into the house. "We have found them, sir; they are all alive!"

" Thank God! thank God!" the farmer exclaimed reverently, and then seeing his wife insensible hurried towards her, uttering a shout for the servants. Two women ran in. "Look to your mistress," he said; "she has fainted; the good news has been too much for her—the boys are found alive."

With mingled exclamations of gladness and dismay the servants raised their mistress.

"Now, boys, where are they?" Mr. Humphreys asked.

The lads gave a rapid narrative of what had happened.

"Under the snow all this time!" the farmer exclaimed; "they must be, as you say, in a hut. Now, will one of you stay and show me the way back, and the others go on to Mr. Jackson's and other places, and bring a strong party of men with shovels on after us?"

The lad who had spoken with the prisoners remained to act as guide, the others hurried off.

"Come with me, my boy, into the larder. There, help yourself; you must be hungry and tired, and you have got to do it over again."

Mr. Humphreys then ran into the yard, and bade the four labourers provide themselves with shovels and prepare to accompany him at once.

He then went back into the parlour. His wife was just opening her eyes; for a time she looked confused and bewildered, then suddenly she sat up and gazed beseechingly at her husband—memory had come back to her.

" Yes, wife, thanks be to God, it is true—the boys are alive ; I am just going with these men to dig them out. They are snowed up in a hut. Now, Jane, get a large basket, and put in it lots of bread and bacon — the men who are working will want something ; fill the largest stone jar with beer ; put in a bottle of brandy and a bottle of milk, and set to and get some soup ready ; bring three small mattresses downstairs and a lot of blankets."

Five minutes later the search-party started, Mr. Humphreys and the guide leading the way ; the men followed, one carrying five shovels ; another, the basket and jar ; the other two, three hurdles on which were placed the mattresses and blankets.

It was no easy matter so laden making their way over the hills and through the deep drifts. Mr. Humphreys took his share of the labour ; but it was two hours from the time when they started before they arrived at the spot where the flag was waving, and the night was already closing in.

Mr. Humphreys hurried forward to the flag ; he knelt down beside it.

" Are you still alive, Dick ?—it is I, your father ! "

" Yes, father, we are all alive, and we shall be all right now you have come. Don't get too near the stick ; we are afraid of the hole closing up, and smothering us."

" Which side is the door," Mr. Humphreys asked, " so that we can dig that way ? "

"There is no door, father; but you had better dig from below, because of the wall."

"There must be a door," Mr. Humphreys said to himself, as he rejoined the men. "There can't be a hut without a door; Dick must be a little light-headed, and no wonder. Now, lads, let us set to work from below."

The five men were soon at work, throwing aside the snow. In a short time the other parties arrived.

Mr. Humphreys had brought with him a stock of candles. These were lit and stuck in the snow, where, as there was no wind, they burnt steadily, affording sufficient light for the search. The work was all the more difficult from the lightness of the snow, as the sides fell in like sand as they worked upon it, and they were obliged to make a very broad cutting.

At last there was a cheer, as they struck the ground.

"Now, working up hill we must be at the hut in a few feet."

Twenty willing hands laboured away incessantly, but to their surprise no hut was met with; they worked and worked, throwing the snow behind them, until Mr. Jackson struck his shovel upon something hard.

"Here is a wall or something," he said.

Another minute uncovered a low wall of two feet in height, and directly afterwards a leg was popped up through the snow. A loud cheer broke from the men.

But again the snow-drift fell in from the sides, and it was another quarter of an hour before the lads were lifted from the narrow shelter where they had for **five** days lain.

The Jacksons were too weak to stand, but Dick was just able to keep on his feet. A cup of milk mixed with some brandy was given to each. Then Dick in a few words told the story, and the surprise of all, as they examined the little hut and heard the details of the almost miraculous preservation of the boys, was almost unbounded.

They were now wrapped in blankets and laid on mattresses placed on the hurdles ; the contents of the baskets—for others besides Mr. Humphreys had brought a stock of provisions, not knowing how long the search-party might be engaged—were distributed among the workers, and then four men lifted each hurdle and the party started for home, a messenger having been sent back at full speed directly the boys were got out, to bear the glad news to Castleton.

It was just midnight when the main body returned. A second cup of brandy and milk had done much to revive the two elder boys, and Dick had been able to eat a piece of bread. James, however, had fallen asleep directly he was wrapped in the blankets, and did not awake until he was set down at his father's door.

At both houses doctors were in waiting for their arrival. Dick was at once pronounced to be none the worse for his adventure, except that his feet were frost-bitten from long contact with the snow ; indeed had it not been from this cause he could, on the following day, have been up and about. As it was, in a fortnight, he was perfectly himself again.

Tom Jackson was confined to the house for many weeks; he lost several of his toes, but eventually became strong and hearty again. James, however, never recovered—the shock to his system had been too great; he lingered on for some months, and then sank quietly and painlessly.

The events of the snow-storm left a far deeper trace upon Mrs. Humphreys than upon her son. The terrible anxiety of those five days had told greatly upon her, and after they were over she seemed to lose strength rapidly. She had never been very strong, and a hacking cough now constantly shook her. The doctor who attended her looked serious, and one day said to Mr. Humphreys,—

"I don't like the state of your wife; she has always been weak in her lungs, and I fear that the anxiety she went through has somehow accentuated her former tendency to consumption. The air of this place—you see she was born in the south—is too keen for her. If I were you I would take her up to London and consult some first-rate man in lung diseases, and get his opinion."

The next day Mr. Humphreys started for London. The celebrated physician examined his wife, and afterwards took him aside.

"I cannot conceal from you," he said, "that your wife's lungs are very seriously affected, although consumption has not yet thoroughly set in. If she remains in this country she may not live many months; your only hope is to take her abroad—could you do that?"

"Yes, sir," Mr. Humphreys said. "I can take her anywhere. Where would you advise?"

"She would benefit from a residence either in Egypt or Madeira," the doctor said; "but for a permanency I should say the Cape. I have known many complete cures made there. You tell me that you are engaged in agricultural pursuits; if it is possible for you to settle there, I can give you every hope of saving her life, as the disease is not yet developed. If you go, don't stay in the lowlands, but get up into the high plateaus, either behind the Cape itself, or behind Natal. The climate there is delicious, and land cheap."

Mr. Humphreys thanked him and left, returning the next day to Castleton. The astonishment of the boys, and indeed of Mrs. Humphreys, was unbounded, when the farmer announced in the evening at supper that he intended to sell his land and emigrate at once to the Cape.

The boys were full of excitement at the new and strange idea, and asked numerous questions, none of which the farmer could answer; but he brought out a pile of books, which he had purchased in town, concerning the colonies and their resources, and for once Dick's aversion to books vanished, and he was soon as much absorbed as his brother in the perusal of the accounts of the new land to which they were to go.

On the following Saturday, to the surprise of all Castleton, an advertisement appeared in the Derbyshire paper announcing the sale by auction at an early date of Mr. Humphreys' farm.

Dick and John were quite heroes among their companions, who looked with envy at boys who were going to live in a land where lions and elephants and all sorts of wild beasts abounded, to say nothing of warlike natives.

"There always seem to be Kaffir wars going on," one boy said, "out at the Cape ; you will have all sorts of excitement, Dick."

"I don't think that sort of excitement will be nice," Dick replied; "it must be horribly anxious work to think every time you go out to work that the place may be attacked and every one killed before you get back. But that is all nonsense, you know ; I have been reading about some of the Kaffir wars ; they are in the bush-country, down by the sea. We are going up on to the high lands at the back of Natal. Father says very likely we may buy a farm in the Transvaal, but mother does not seem to like the accounts of the Dutchmen or Boers, as they are called, who live there, and says she would rather have English neighbours ; so I expect if we can get a farm somewhere in the Natal colony, we shall do so."

"You seem to know all about the place," the boy said, surprised.

"Well, we have had seven or eight books to read about it, and I seem now to know more about South

Africa than about any other country in the world.
There are the diamond-fields, too, out there, and
I hope, before I settle down regularly to a farm,
that father will let me go for a few months and try
my luck there. Would it not just be jolly to find a
diamond as big as a pigeon's egg and worth about
twenty thousand pounds?"

"And do they do that?" the boy asked.

"Well, they don't often find them as big as that;
still, one might be the lucky one."

The news that Mr. Humphreys and his family
were about to sell off and emigrate naturally caused
a great deal of talk in and around Castleton, and
put the idea into the minds of many who had never
before seriously thought of it. If Mr. Humphreys,
who had one of the best farms in the neighbourhood,
thought that it would pay him to sell his land and go
out, it would surely be a good thing for others to
do the same. He was considered to be a good
farmer and a long-headed man; one who would
not take such a step without carefully looking into
the matter—for Mr. Humphreys, in order to avoid
questioning and the constant inquiries about his
wife's health, which would be made, did he announce
that he was leaving for that reason, did not think it
necessary to inform people that it was in the hopes
of staving off the danger which threatened her that
he was making a move.

A great many of the neighbouring labourers
would gladly have gone with him; but he found by

his reading that Kaffir labour was to be obtained
out there very cheaply. He determined, however, to
take with him two of his own hands; the one a strong
active young fellow named Bill Harrison, the other a
middle-aged man named Johnson, who had been
with him from a boy. He was a married man
with two girls, aged fifteen and sixteen, the eldest
of whom was already employed by Mrs. Humphreys
in the house. Johnson's wife was a superior woman
of her class, and Mr. Humphreys thought that it
would be pleasant for his wife, having a woman
at hand, whom she could speak to. The girls
were to act as servants—indeed Mr. Humphreys
thought it probable that the whole party would
live under one roof.

Among those whom Mr. Humphreys' decision to
emigrate had much moved was Mr. Jackson. He
was not in so good a position, as he did not farm
his own land; but he had sufficient capital to start
him well in the colony, where a farm can be bought
outright at a few shillings an acre. He talked the
matter over with his friend on several occasions,
and at last said,—

"Well, I think I have pretty well made up my
mind; the doctor is telling me that my poor little
chap is not likely to live long; his mother is wrapped
up in him, and will never like the place again;—so I
think on all grounds a change will be good. I can't
come out with you, because I have got a lease of
the farm; but I fancy that it is worth more than it

was when I took it, and if I can get a good tenant to take it off my hands I don't suppose the landlord will make any objections. I shall look about at once, and, when my poor little chap is gone, I shan't be long before I come after you. You will let me know how you find the place, and whether these book-accounts are true?—I have heard that many of these chaps who write books are awful liars. I should like to get a farm as near you as may be."

It was early in the spring when Mr. Humphreys and his party embarked at Plymouth in the *Dunster Castle*. The farm had sold well, and Mr. Humphreys possessed a capital of several thousand pounds—a sum which would make him a rich man in the colony. None of the party had ever seen the sea before, and the delight of the two boys and the wonderment of the labourers at all they saw was very great. Mr. Humphreys had taken first-class passages for himself and family, while the others of course were steerage passengers.

CHAPTER III.

THE FARM.

THE voyage to the Cape passed without any incident whatever. The weather was fine the whole distance. Without even a single storm to break the monotony they touched at Capetown and Port Elizabeth, and at last arrived at Durban. The journey had not been too long for the boys; everything was so perfectly new to them that they were never tired of watching the sea and looking for porpoises and the shoals of fish, over which hovered thousands of birds.

Once or twice they saw a whale spout, while flying-fish were matters of hourly occurrence. They had prodigious appetites, and greatly enjoyed the food, which was altogether different to that to which they had been accustomed. They had stopped at Madeira and St. Vincent, where great stocks of delicious fruit had been taken on board. Altogether they were quite sorry when they arrived at the end of the voyage.

The landing was effected in large boats, as the *Dunster Castle* drew too much water to cross the bar at the mouth of the harbour.

They stopped only one day at Durban, where Mr. Humphreys hired a waggon to take the party to

Pieter-Maritzburg, the capital. He was not encumbered with baggage, as he had decided to buy everything he wanted in the colony.

"You may pay dearer," he said, "no doubt; but then you get just what you want. If I were to take out implements, they might not be suited to the requirements of the country. As for clothes, they would of course be pretty much the same everywhere; still, it is better to take out only a year's requirements and to buy as we want, instead of lumbering over the country with a quantity of heavy baggage."

The party were greatly amused at their first experience of a Cape waggon; it was of very large size, massively built, and covered with a great tilt; and it was drawn by sixteen oxen, spanned two by two. This was an altogether unnecessary number for the weight which had to be carried, but the waggon had come down loaded from the interior, and Mr. Humphreys therefore paid no more than he would have done for a waggon with a small number of oxen. They took two days to accomplish the journey, the women sleeping at night in the waggon, and Mr. Humphreys and his sons in blankets on the ground.

The driver, who was an Englishman, had been many years in the colony, and from him, upon the road, Mr. Humphreys gained much valuable information about the country. The driver was assisted by two Kaffirs, one of whom walked ahead of the leading cattle, the other alongside, shouting and prodding them.

The boys were astonished at the power and accuracy with which the driver whirled his whip; this had a short handle and a lash of twenty yards long, and with it he was able to hit any animal of the team with absolute certainty, and indeed to make the thong alight on any part of their bodies at which he aimed.

On their arrival at Pieter-Maritzburg Mr. Humphreys hired a house, and here he placed his party while he set to work to make inquiries after a suitable location. He soon heard of several places which seemed suitable, and having bought a horse started for Newcastle, a small town situated close to the frontier-line between the Transvaal and Natal.

He was away for three weeks, and on his return informed his wife that he had purchased a farm of 2000 acres, with a substantial farmhouse, at a distance of ten miles from Newcastle, for the sum of 1500*l.*

The farmhouse was already roughly furnished, but Mr. Humphreys purchased a number of other articles, which would make it comfortable and home-like. He laid in a great stock of groceries, and then hiring a waggon, similar to that in which they had before travelled, started with his party for the farm, having also hired four Kaffirs to assist there. Travelling by easy stages, it took them twelve days to get to Newcastle. The country was undulating and the road rose steadily the whole distance.

Near Pieter-Maritzburg the population was comparatively thick. The fields were well cultivated and the vegetation thick and luxuriant, but as they ascended the character of the country changed. Vast stretches of rolling grass everywhere met the eye. This was now beautifully· green, for it was winter. In the summer and autumn the grass becomes dry and burnt up ; fire is then applied to it, and the whole country assumes a black mantle. But the first shower of rain brings up the young grass and in a very short time the country is covered with fresh verdure.

Mr. Humphreys told his wife that, before fixing on the farm, he had ridden into the Transvaal, and found that land could be purchased there even more cheaply than in Natal ; but that he had much conversation with English settlers on the frontier, and these had for the most part strongly advised him to settle inside the Natal frontier.

"It may be that all will be right," one had told him, "but the Boers have not yet recovered from their scare from Secoceni."

"Who is Secoceni, father?" Dick asked. "The books we have say nothing about him."

"No," Mr. Humphreys said ; "they were all published a few years since, and none of them treat much of the affairs of the Transvaal, which, as an independent state, had comparatively little interest to English settlers. There are in the Transvaal, which is of immense extent, a very large number of natives, enormously outnumbering the Boers. In the southern districts, where the Boers are strongest, they cruelly ill-treat the natives, making slaves of them, and thinking no more of shooting one of them down than they would of shooting a dog. In the outlying provinces they live almost on sufferance of the natives, and, were these to unite their forces and rise, they could annihilate the Dutch. Secoceni is a powerful chief, who lives with his tribe in a natural stronghold ; he has always held himself as independent of the Dutch. As his men used to make raids upon the Boers' cattle, the latter attacked him, and in alliance with Swazis, another powerful tribe, endeavoured to carry his fortress ; they were, however, badly beaten ; it being only by the gallantry of their native allies that the Boer contingent was saved from destruction. Secoceni then took the offensive. A perfect panic seized the Boers ; they refused to obey the orders of their government, and to turn out to resist the invaders. The treasury was empty, for their government had never been enabled to persuade them to pay taxes. They applied for aid to Natal, but finally their plight was so bad that they were glad to accept the offer which Mr. Shepstone made them, of annexation to England, by which they secured our protection and were safe from annihilation. Secoceni was not the only enemy who threatened them. They had a still more formidable foe in the Zulus on the eastern frontier. These are a very warlike people, and it was known that their king meditated the conquest of the Transvaal. But, glad enough as the Boers were at the moment to accept the protection of England, now that the danger is over a great many of them would like to kick down the bridge which has helped them over the stream. They make no secret of their dislike to Englishmen, and although they are glad enough to sell their land at prices immensely in advance of the former value, for indeed land was previously almost unsaleable in the Transvaal, they are on bad terms with them. One of my informants describes them as a sullen, sulky people, and predicts that sooner or later we shall have trouble with them ; so I thought it better altogether to pay a little higher for my land, and to be within the boundaries of this colony."

On arriving at the farm Mrs. Humphreys was glad to find that the house, though rough, was substantial. It was built of stone. The walls were of great thickness, as the stones were laid without mortar, with which, however, it was faced inside and out. One large room occupied the greater portion of the ground floor; beside this was a small sitting-room. Upstairs were four bedrooms. For the time the small room downstairs was turned into a bedroom, which Mr. and Mrs. Humphreys occupied. The four bedrooms upstairs just held the rest of the party. The out-houses consisted only of a large barn and a rough stable.

Mr. Humphreys at once rode over to Newcastle, and obtained the services of a mason and six Kaffirs, and proceeded to add a wing to the farmhouse. This was for the use of John on and his wife, and Harrison. The whole party were, however, to take their meals together in the great kitchen. A hut was also built for the Kaffirs, and another large stable was erected.

A few days after his arrival Mr. Humphreys went across the border into the Transvaal, taking Harrison and two of the Kaffirs with him, and returned a fortnight later with a herd of 400 cattle, which he had purchased. He also bought three yoke of oxen, broken to the plough. Hitherto the farm had been purely a pastoral one, but Mr. Humphreys at once began to break up some land for wheat and Indian corn. The Kaffirs were set to work to fence and dig up a plot round the house for vegetables, and to dig holes near it, over a space of some acres, for the reception of 3000 young fruit-trees—apples, pears, peaches, and plums,—which he had bought at Pieter-Maritzburg, and which were to come up in two months' time. He also bought six riding-horses.

In a few weeks the farm assumed quite a different appearance. A gang of Kaffirs, ten strong, had been hired to hurry on the work of preparing the orchard and erecting a fence round it. Wood was, Mr. Humphreys found, extremely scarce and dear, the country being absolutely bare of trees, and wood for fuel was only obtained in kloofs or deep hollows, and had to be fetched long distances.

" I suppose," Mrs. Humphreys said to her husband one evening, " you mean to make cattle-raising your principal point ? "

" No," he said ; " every one raises cattle, and the

Dutch can do it cheaper than we can; they have immense tracts of land, and their Kaffir labour costs them next to nothing. I do not say that we could not live and to a certain extent thrive on cattle, but I think that there is something much better to be done. Wood is an awful price here, and all that is used has to be brought up from the coast. I think therefore of planting trees. The climate is magnificent, and their growth will be rapid. They will of course require fencing to keep out the cattle, but I shall do that, as I am doing the orchard, with wire fencing and light iron-uprights. Labour is plentiful, and there are large nurseries near Pieter-Maritzburg, where I can procure any number of young trees; so I mean to plant 200 acres a year—in ten years the whole farm will be planted, and the loppings for poles and fire-wood will in a very short time after planting begin to pay well. In fifteen years the first 200 acres will be fit to fell, and the property will be worth a very large sum of money. Of course we can sell out before that if we like. But at the present price of wood up here, or even should it fall to a quarter of its present price, the value of the 2000 acres of wood will in twenty years be extremely large."

The boys were delighted with their new life. Mr. Humphreys had, before leaving England, bought for Dick a Winchester repeating-rifle. These arms are very light, and Dick was able to carry his without difficulty; and very shortly after their arrival his father had a mark erected at a distance from the house, at which he could practise with safety. Game was abundant all over the country. Herds of deer and antelope of various kinds often swept past in sight of the farmhouse, and winged game also abounded.

Mr. Humphreys had at home been considered a first-rate shot at partridges, and had for four or five years belonged to the Castleton volunteers, and had carried off many prizes for rifle-shooting. He was now able, by going out for a few hours once or twice a week, to keep the larder well supplied, and the little flock of fifty sheep, which he had bought for home-consumption, was but seldom drawn upon. The Kaffirs were fed upon mealies, as they call Indian corn, of which Mr. Humphreys had no difficulty in purchasing sufficient for his wants from the neighbouring farmers.

His next neighbours were two brothers, Scotchmen, named Fraser, who lived at a distance of four miles. They rode over the day after the travellers' arrival, and offered their services in any way. Mr. Humphreys, however, was well supplied with stores of all kinds, and his two white labourers, being both handy men, were able to do all that was required about the house.

The Frasers proved pleasant neighbours, and often rode over and spent Sunday with the Humphreys, and the boys sometimes went over and spent the day with them.

A Kaffir lad, son of one of the men engaged upon

the farm, was hired by Mr. Humphreys as a 'special attendant for Dick.   On these vast undulating plains, where there are no trees to serve as a landmark, it is exceedingly difficult for a stranger to find his way.   Dick was told by his father that, whether riding or walking, he was always to take the Kaffir boy with him ; and except when he was indulging in a gallop the lad was easily able to keep up with him. He had been born a hunter, and soon taught Dick how to stalk the timid deer, and, as the lad improved in his shooting, he was ere long enabled to keep the larder supplied—a duty which Mr. Humphreys gladly handed over to him, as every minute of his own time was occupied by his work on the farm.

Of an evening after supper, which was partaken of at the conclusion of work, the men retired to their own wing and Mrs. Humphreys and the two girls sat down to their sewing by the fire ; for upon the uplands the evenings are quite cold enough to find a fire a comfort in winter.   Then the boys would take out their lesson-books and work steadily for three hours.   Under the changed conditions of their life, Mr. Humphreys felt that Dick might, if he chose, well discontinue his study of the classics, and his work therefore consisted in the reading of history, travels, and books of scientific knowledge.

"Next to being a learned man," his father said to him, "the best and most useful thing is to be a thoroughly well-informed man on all general subjects."

John, however, continued his studies as before ; his life of outdoor exercise strengthened and improved him, and he no longer wished to be always sitting with a book in his hand—still, he had a natural love of study, which his father encouraged, deeming it possible that as he grew up he might be unwilling to embrace the life of a colonist, in which case he determined to send him home to finish his education in England, and afterwards to start him in any profession he might select.

Finding that the cost of carriage up the country was very high, and as he would yearly require many wag-gon-loads of young trees and fencing Mr. Humphreys determined to do his own teaming ; he therefore bought two of the large country-waggons and set a Kaffir to work to break in some young steers to the yoke.

Six months after their arrival in the colony they had for the first time visitors to stay at the farm—Mr. Jackson, his wife, his son Tom, and two daughters com-ing out to settle near them. This was a great delight to the boys, and fortunately Mr. Jackson was able to buy a farm of 500 acres adjoining that of his friend ; the house, however, was but a cabin, and while a fresh one was being erected the family remained guests of the Humphreys. Mr. Jackson had, at his friend's advice, brought with him from England a labourer with his wife and family, who at once took up their residence in the hut on the farm.

To Dick the coming of the Jacksons was a source of special pleasure. Tom was just his own age, and the two boys had become inseparable friends at home after their adventure in the snow, upon which occasion Tom, as he freely owned, had owed his life to Dick's energy and promptness of suggestion. Dick was fond of his brother, but three years make a great difference at this period of life, and, as their tastes were wholly dissimilar, John had never been a companion for him. Since their arrival in South Africa they had got on very well together; still, they had not the same ideas or subjects of thought, and it was an immense delight to Dick to have his old friend and companion with him.

It must not be supposed that Dick's time was occupied solely in amusement; from early morning until dinner-time he worked steadily. Sometimes he assisted to erect the hurdles and strain the wires of the fencing; at others he aided in the planting of the fruit-trees; then he would be with the Kaffirs who were breaking in the oxen for the waggons. At all times he took off his coat and worked with the rest, for, as his father said,—

"If a farmer is to be able properly to look after men at work, he must be able to do the work himself."

While Dick was at work with the men, John, who was too young to be of any use, remained indoors at his books, and, although of an afternoon he would stroll out, he seldom went far from the house. The other boys generally went for long rides when work was done. One day they sighted a herd of steinbock. Leaving their horses with the Kaffir lad in a hollow, they crept round so as to get the deer between them and the wind, and managed to reach unobserved a brow within a hundred yards of the herd. Dick had by this time become a good shot, and the buck at which he aimed fell dead in its tracks. Tom was not much of a shot, but he had fired into the thick of the deer and gave a shout of delight at seeing one of them fall. The rest of the herd dashed off at full speed. Tom ran, shouting, forward, but to his mortification the stag that he had hit rose again to its feet and went off at a trot in the direction taken by the others ; a minute later the Kaffir boy was seen running towards them at his full speed, leading the horses.

The two boys on his arrival leapt into their saddles and started in pursuit of the wounded stag, which was still in sight, thinking at first they could easily ride it down. But the animal seemed rather to gain than to lose strength, and, although they had considerably lessened the start he had obtained of them, he still kept steadily on. Active and wiry as their horses were, they could not overtake it, and the boys had at last the mortification of seeing that the stag was now gaining upon them, and they presently drew rein, and their panting horses came to a standstill.

"What a horrid sell!" Tom Jackson exclaimed angrily. "I can't understand his going like that after I fairly brought him down."

"I expect," Dick said, "that your bullet can only have grazed his skull ; it stunned him for the moment, but after he had once come to himself he went on as briskly as usual. If he had been hard hit we should certainly have ridden him down."

"Well, I suppose," Tom said more goodhumouredly, "there is nothing for it but to ride back."

"But which is our road?" Dick said in some dismay. "I am sure I have no idea, and now that the sun is gone in there is nothing to steer by."

While they had been riding, the day had changed; the sky, which had for weeks been bright and fine, was now overcast with heavy clouds.

"We are in for a storm, I think," Dick went on, "and it is coming on fast. I have not an idea which way to go, and I think our best plan will be to halt. Joel will track us, and the farther we go the longer he will be in overtaking us. There is the first drop! The best thing to do, Tom, will be to take off our saddles and tether our horses, and then to wait. This storm is a nuisance; in the first place we shall be drenched, in the second it will wash out our tracks, and the darkness will come so quickly that I am afraid Joel will not be able to trace us. You see we do not know whether we have been riding straight or not; the stag may have been running in a circle for anything we know, and as we have been riding for something like two hours, we may be within five miles of home or we may be five and twenty."

Scarcely had the boys got the saddles off and tethered their horses when the rain came down in a sheet, accompanied by the most tremendous thunder and the most vivid lightning Tom had ever seen.

"This is awful, Dick," he said.

"Yes," Dick agreed; "thunderstorms here are frightful. Houses are often struck; but, lying down here in the open, there is not much fear."

For hours the storm continued unabated; the rain came down in a perfect deluge. The boys had put their saddles together and had covered these with the horse-cloths so as to form a sort of tent, but they were nevertheless soaked to the skin, and, to add to their discomfiture, the horses had been so frightened by the blinding glare of the lightning that they tugged at the ropes until, as the wet penetrated the ground, the pegs became loosened, and they scoured away into the darkness.

After continuing for five hours the rain suddenly ceased.

"What are we to do in the morning, Dick?"

"If it is fine it will be easy enough; we shall put our saddles on our heads and walk eastward. I have got a little pocket-compass which father gave me in case I should at any time get lost, so we shall have no difficulty in keeping our way, and sooner or later we must strike the road running north to Newcastle."

They did not, however, wait till morning; so wet and chilled were they, that they agreed they would rather walk than lie still. Accordingly they put the saddles on their heads as soon as the rain ceased and the stars shone out, struck a light and looked at their compass, fixed on a star to steer by, and then set out on their journey.

Fortunately, after two hours' walking, they struck the road at a point some ten miles from the farm, and were home soon after daybreak, just as their fathers were about to set out with a body of Kaffirs in search of them. Joel had returned late at night, having turned his face homeward when it became too dark to follow the track; the horses had both come in during the night.

CHAPTER IV.

THE OUTBREAK OF WAR.

As soon as the Jacksons' house was finished, they went into residence there; but two or three times a week Dick and Tom managed to meet, one or other being sure to find some excuse for riding over.

The Humphreys had arrived in Natal at the end of April, 1877, and by November in the following year their farm presented a very different appearance to that which it had worn on their arrival—sixteen months of energetic labour, carried on by a considerable number of hands, will effect wonders. Possessing ample capital Mr. Humphreys was able to keep a strong gang of Kaffirs at work, and for some time had thirty men upon the farm. Thus the house which, when he took it, stood solitary and lone in a bare plain, was now surrounded by 200 acres of young trees. Of these, twenty acres were fruit-trees; the remainder, trees grown for their wood. These were planted thickly, as they would every year be thinned out, and the young poles would fetch a good sum for fencing. Although they had only been planted a few months, they were already green and bright; they were protected from the cattle by a wire fence encircling the whole.

The cattle had thriven and were doing well, and a large field of Indian corn had been harvested for the use of the Kaffirs. The cattle had nearly doubled in numbers, as Mr. Humphreys did not care about selling at present. The expenses of living were slight. Meat, fowls, and eggs were raised upon the farm, and the guns of Mr. Humphreys and Dick provided them with a plentiful supply of game. Four milch cows were kept in a paddock near the house, and supplied it with milk, butter, and cheese. Groceries and flour had alone to be purchased, and, as Mr. Humphreys said, he did not care if he did not sell a head of cattle for the next ten years ; but he would be obliged to do so before long, as the farm would carry but a small number more than he already possessed, and its available extent for that purpose would diminish every year, as the planting went on.

Mr. Humphreys was fortunate in having a small stream run through his farm. He erected a dam across a hollow, so that in winter a pond of two or three acres in extent, and fifteen or sixteen feet deep, was formed, affording an ample supply for the summer ; this was of great utility to him, as he was thereby enabled to continue his planting operations, filling up each hole with water when the trees were put in, and then, as this subsided, filling in the eaith ; by this means the young trees got a good start, and seldom required watering afterwards. He had a large water-cart built for him ; this was drawn by four oxen, and brought the water to the point where the Kaffirs were engaged in planting.

Steers sufficient for two waggons had been broken

in, and when these were not employed in bringing up young trees and fencing from Newcastle they worked upon the road between Newcastle and Pieter-Maritzburg, there being a great demand for conveyance, as numbers of traders were going up into the Transvaal and opening stores there. Mr. Jackson had also two waggons engaged in the same work. When trees and goods were wanted for the farm, Dick went down with the waggons to see that these were properly loaded, and that the young trees, which were often in leaf, were taken out every night and set with the roots in water until the morning.

One evening, early in October, Mr. Jackson rode over with Tom.

"I have heard," the former said to Mr. Humphreys, "that the government have determined on moving the troops down to the Zulu frontier; the attitude of Cetewayo is very threatening."

"He is a troublesome neighbour," Mr. Humphreys said. "They say that he has 30,000 fighting-men, and in that case he ought to be able to overrun both Natal and the Transvaal, for there is no doubt that Zulus fight with great bravery. As for the Dutch, I really can't blame the Zulus. The Boers are always encroaching on their territory, and any remonstrance is answered by a rifle-shot. Had it not been for our annexation of the Transvaal, Cetewayo would have overrun it and exterminated the Dutch before now. We have a strong force in the colony just at present, and I think Sir Bartle Frere means to bring matters

E

to a crisis. The existence of such an army of warlike savages on the frontier is a standing threat to the very existence of the colony, and the constitution of the army renders it almost a necessity that it should fight. All the men are soldiers, and as none are allowed to marry until the regiment to which they belong has distinguished itself in battle they are naturally always burning for war. The Pieter-Maritzburg paper says that it understands that Sir Bartle Frere is about to send in an ultimatum, demanding—in addition to various small matters, such as the punishing of raiders across the frontier—the entire abandonment of the present system of the Zulu army, and cessation of the bloody massacres which constantly take place in that country. If a man offends the king, not only is he put to death, but the whole of the people of his village are often massacred. Altogether an abominable state of things prevails; there seems to be but one opinion throughout the colony, that it is absolutely necessary for our safety that the Zulu organization shall be broken up."

"I see," Mr. Jackson said, "that there is an advertisement in the papers for waggons for the transport of stores, and the price offered is excellent. A large number are required; I was thinking of sending down my two teams—what do you think?"

"I have been turning it over in my mind," Mr. Humphreys replied, "and I am inclined also to offer my waggons. The rate of pay is, as you say, high, and they certainly will have a difficulty in obtaining the number they require. I shall not have need for mine for home purposes for a considerable time now. The hot weather will soon be setting in, and planting is over for the season. I shall of course go on digging holes for my next batch, but I shall not want them up until after the end of the hot season. So I think, as I can spare them, I shall hire them to government. I think we ought all to do what we can to aid it at present, for every one agrees as to the necessity of the steps it is now taking."

"And do you think that there will be any fighting, father?" Dick asked eagerly.

"That no one can say, my boy. The Zulus are a proud as well as a brave people, and believe that they are invincible. I hardly think that they will consent to break up their army and abandon their customs at our dictation; I should not be surprised if it comes to fighting."

"Oh, father, if you hire the waggons to government, may I go with them? I can see that the Kaffirs look after the oxen, you know, and that everything goes straight. I have picked up a little Kaffir from Joel, and can manage to make them understand."

"Well, Dick," Mr. Humphreys said, after a little thought, "I don't know that I have any objection to it; it will be a change for you, and of course there will be no chance of the waggons being near if any fighting goes on. What do you think, Jackson? I suppose your boy will want to go if mine does?"

"Well, I don't mind," Mr. Jackson answered. "I suppose it will not be for long, for the boy is useful on the farm now. However, as you say, it will be a change, and boys like a little excitement. Well, I suppose I must say yes; they are fifteen now, and old enough to keep out of mischief."

The boys were delighted at the prospect of the expedition, and at once went out to talk matters over together. They cordially agreed in the hope that the Zulus would fight, and promised themselves that if possible they would see something of it. Their fathers would, they thought, allow them to take their horses, and it would be easy, if the waggons were left behind, to ride forward with the troops, and see what went on.

Two days later the four teams started together for Pieter-Maritzburg. Contrary to their expectations the boys were not allowed to take their horses.

"No, no, Dick," Mr. Humphreys had said, when his son asked him, "no horses, if you please; I know what you will be up to. Galloping about to see what is going on, and getting into all sorts of mischief and scrapes. No, if you go, you go with the waggons, to see that everything goes straight, to translate orders to the Kaffirs, and to learn something of waggon-driving across a rough country. For between this place and Pieter-Maritzburg it is such a fair road that you really learn nothing in that way; once get into a cross country, and you will see how they get waggons down steep kloofs, across streams, and over rough places. No, you and Tom will stick to the waggons. I have been fixing a number of rings to-day underneath one of them, and your mother and the women have been at work, making a sort of curtain to hook on all round; so at night you will have a comfortable place to sleep in, for the waggons will likely enough be so filled with cases and stores that there will be no sleeping in them. You can take the double-barrel as well as your Winchester, as of an evening you may be able to get a shot sometimes at game, which will vary your rations a bit. You must take with you a stock of tinned meats from Pieter-Maritzburg, for I do not suppose they will issue regular rations to you. So long as you are this side of the Tugela, you will be able to buy food; but if the troops cross into Zululand, you may have to depend on what you carry."

Tom with his two waggons arrived at daybreak, and the four teams set off together, Mrs. Humphreys —who had now completely lost her cough and was quite strong and well—laying many injunctions upon Dick against exposing himself to any danger, and Dick promising to be as careful as possible.

Upon their arrival at Pieter-Maritzburg the boys went at once to the government transport-yard, and on stating their errand were shown into the office of the officer in charge.

"We have brought down four teams of sixteen oxen

each," Dick said, "from near Newcastle, to be hired to the government."

"That is right, my lads," the officer said, "we have room for plenty more. This is the form of contract. You engage to serve the government by the month; you bear any damages which may take place from wear and tear of the roads, breakdowns, and the other ordinary accidents of travel; the government engages to make good any loss or damage which may occur from the action of the enemy. This is not," he said, smiling, "likely to take place, but still those are the terms. Have you any authority from your fathers, to whom, I suppose, the teams belong, to sign the contracts for them?"

"Yes, sir," Dick said. "Here is a paper from my father, and one from Tom Jackson's father, saying that they agree to be bound by the terms of the contract, and that they authorize us to sign in their names. We are going with the waggons, sir, to look after the Kaffirs."

"Well," the officer said, "you can do as you like about that; but if you speak Kaffir it will be useful— only, mind, you will have to provision yourselves. From the day the teams are taken up, rations of mealies will be served to the Kaffirs at the various halting-places, but there is no provision for rations of white men. The cattle, too, will be fed, but you will have to see to yourselves."

"Yes, sir; we expected to do so."

"Well, you had better fetch the teams up to the

yard. I must inspect and pass them before they are taken up. Bring them round at once; then they will be loaded to-night, and start at daybreak to-morrow."

The teams were brought round to the yard, and immediately passed by the officer, who indeed remarked upon the excellence of the animals. The Kaffirs were directed to outspan or unyoke the oxen, for whom rations of hay and grain were at once issued.

The boys returned to the town and made their purchases, which were carried down by two Kaffirs and stored in the waggons, which were already in process of being loaded—two with boxes of ammunition, the others with miscellaneous stores for the troops. They slept at an hotel, and next morning at daybreak presented themselves at the yard. The Kaffirs were already harnessing up the oxen, and in a quarter of an hour the four waggons, with sixteen others, started for the Tugela.

It was now the middle of December. Early in the month commissioners had been sent to Cetewayo with the terms decided upon by Sir Bartle Frere. The first clauses of the document contained the settlement of the disputed frontier, and fines were fixed to be paid by the chiefs whose men had committed forays across the borders; it then went on to demand that the whole of Cetewayo's army should at once be disbanded; freedom of marriage was to be allowed, when the parties thereto were of age; justice was to be impartially administered; missionaries to be allowed to reside in the Zulu country; British residents to be appointed; all disputes between Zulus and Europeans to be referred to the king and resident; and no expulsion from Zulu territory was to be carried into effect without the distinct approval of the resident.

It was intimated to the king that unless these terms were accepted by the 11th of January the army would at once invade the country. Few men expected that the Zulu king would tamely submit to conditions which would deprive him of all the military power in which he delighted, and would reduce him to a state of something like dependency upon the British.

During the month of December General Thesiger, who commanded the British forces in South Africa, made every effort to prepare for hostilities. The regiments which were at the Cape were brought round by sea; a brigade of seamen and marines was landed from the ships of war; several corps of irregular horse were raised among the colonists; and regiments of natives were enrolled. Before the date by which the king was to send in his answer the troops were assembled along the frontier in the following disposition :—

No. 1 Column.

(Headquarters, Thring's Post, Lower Tugela.)
Commandant.—Col. C. K. Pearson, the Buffs.
Naval Brigade.—170 bluejackets and marines of

H.M.S. *Active* (with one Gatling and two 7-pounder guns), under Captain Campbell, R.N.

Royal Artillery.—Two 7-pounder guns and rocket-battery, under Lieut. W. N. Lloyd, R.A.

Infantry.—2nd battalion, 3rd Buffs, under Lieut. Col. H. Parnell.

Mounted Infantry.—100 men under Capt. Barrow, 19th Hussars.

Volunteers.—Durban Rifles, Natal Hussars, Stanger Rifles, Victoria Rifles, Alexandra Rifles. Average, forty men per corps—all mounted.

Native Contingent.—1000 men under Major Graves, the Buffs.

No. 2 Column.

(*Headquarters, Helpmakaar, near Rorke's Drift.*)

Commandant.—Col. Glyn, 1st battalion, 24th Regiment.

Royal Artillery.—N. battery, 5th brigade, Royal Artillery (with 7-pounder guns), under Major A. Harness, R.A.

Infantry.—Seven companies 1st battalion, 24th Regiment, and 2nd battalion, 24th Regiment, under Lieut.-Col. Degacher.

Natal Mounted Police.—Commanded by Major Dartnell.

Volunteers.—Natal Carabineers, Buffalo Border Guard, Newcastle Mounted Rifles—all mounted; average, forty men.

Native Contingent.—1000 men, under Commandant Lonsdale, late 74th Highlanders.

No. 3 COLUMN.
(*Headquarters, Utrecht.*)

Commandant.—Col. Evelyn Wood, V.C. C.B., 40th Regiment.

Royal Artillery.—11th battery, 7th brigade, R.A. (with four 7-pounder guns), under Major E. Tremlett, R.A.

Infantry.—1st battalion 13th Regiment, and 90th Regiment.

Mounted Infantry.—100 men, under Major J. C. Russell, 12th Lancers.

Frontier Light Horse.—200 strong, under Major Redvers Buller, C.B., 60th Rifles.

Volunteers.—The Kaffrarian Vanguard, Commandant Schermbuicker, 100 strong.

Native Contingent.—The Swazis, our native allies, some 5000 strong.

In the first fortnight of their engagement the waggons travelled backward and forward between Pieter-Maritzburg and Grey Town, which for the time formed the base for the column of Colonel Glyn. The distance of the town from the capital was forty-five miles, and as the waggons travelled at the rate of fifteen miles a day, they were twelve days in accomplishing two double journeys. When they were loaded up the third time, they received orders to go straight through to the headquarters of the column at Heipmakaar. The boys were pleased at the change, for the road as far as Grey Town was a good one.

They reached Grey Town for the third time on the

2nd of January. Here they found the place in a state of great excitement, a mounted messenger having arrived that morning with the news that Cetewayo had refused all demands and that large bodies of the Zulus were marching towards the frontier to oppose the various columns collecting there.

On arriving at the government-yard the lads received orders at once to unload the waggons and to take on the stores of the 2nd battalion of the 24th, which was to march from Grey Town the next morning. The start was delayed until the afternoon, as sufficient waggons had not arrived to take on their baggage. The road was rough, and it was late in the afternoon before they arrived at the Mooin River.

The weather had set in wet, the river was in flood, and the oxen had immense difficulty in getting the waggons across. Two teams had to be attached to each waggon, and even then it was as much as they could do to get across, for the water was so high that it nearly took them off their feet.

The troops were taken over in punts, and, after crossing, a halt was made for the night.

After seeing the cattle outspanned and attended to, the boys wandered away among the troops, as they were to start at daybreak, and it was long past dark before all were over. The tents were not pitched, and the troops bivouacked in the open. Brushwood was collected from the rough ground around, and blazing fires were soon burning merrily. It was all new and very amusing to the boys. The troops were in high spirits at the prospect of an early brush with the enemy, and songs were sung around the fires until the bugle rang out the order, " Lights out," when the men wrapped themselves in their blankets and lay down, and the boys retired to their snug shelter under the waggons, where their Kaffirs had as usual laid piles of brushwood to serve as their beds.

The next morning they were off early, and reached the Tugela after five hours' march. This river does not here form the frontier between Zululand and Natal, this being marked by the Buffalo—a much larger and more important stream—from the point where this falls into the Tugela, some fifteen miles below the spot where they crossed the latter river, which here runs towards the southwest.

Two more days' marching took the column to Helpmakaar. The weather was wet and misty, and the troops now marched in close order, with flankers thrown out, for the road ran parallel with the Buffalo, about five miles distant, and it was thought possible that the Zulus might cross the river and commence hostilities. A cordon of sentinels had, however, been placed all along the river from Rorke's Drift down to the point of junction of the Buffalo and Tugela ; below the stream was so wide that there was no fear of the Zulus effecting a crossing.

Most of the troops which had been stationed at Helpmakaar had already marched up to Rorke's Drift, and after staying two days at Help- makaar the 2nd battalion of the 24th marched

to that place, where the 1st battalion of the same
regiment were already encamped.

Two days later the remainder of the force destined
to act under Colonel Glyn had assembled at Rorke's
Drift—the term " drift " meaning a ford across a
river.

This column was the strongest of those which had
been formed for the simultaneous invasion of Zululand, and General Thesiger was himself upon the
spot to accompany it. Many of the waggons which
had brought up stores were sent back to Grey Town
for further supplies; but those of the boys, being
laden with the spare ammunition and baggage of a
portion of the 24th, were to accompany the column in
its advance.

The last two days of the term granted to Cetewayo
to accede to our terms were full of excitement; it had
been reported, indeed, that the king was determined
upon resistance, but it was thought probable that he
might yield at the last moment, and the road leading
down to the drift on the other side of the river was
anxiously watched.

As the hours went on and no messenger was seen
approaching, the spirits of the troops rose, for there
is nothing that soldiers hate so much as, after enduring
the fatigues preparatory to the opening of a campaign, the long marches, the wet nights, and other
privations and hardships, for the enemy to yield without a blow. Men who had been in the campaigns of
Abyssinia and Ashanti told their comrades how on

both occasions the same uncertainty had prevailed as to the intentions of the enemy up to the last moment, and the fact that in both campaigns the enemy had at the last moment resolved to fight, was hailed as a sort of presage that a similar determination would be arrived at by the Zulu king.

To the boys these days passed very pleasantly; they had nothing to do but to wander about the camp and watch the proceedings. There was a parade of the two native regiments before the general, who was much pleased with their appearance, and who exhorted them on no account to kill women, children, or prisoners.

Among these native regiments were curiously many Zulus; for great numbers of this people had at various times been obliged to take refuge in Natal, to avoid the destruction threatened them by their despotic king, and these were now eager to fight against their late monarch.

Some of the bodies of volunteer horse were very smart and soldier-like in their appearance. They were for the most part composed of young farmers, and Dick and Tom bitterly regretted that they had not been a few years older, in which case, instead of looking after a lot of bulls, as Dick contemptuously said, they might have been riding in the ranks of the volunteers.

By the regulars the two days were spent in cleaning their arms and accoutrements, whose burnish and cleanliness had suffered much in the long wet march, and from the bivouacs on the damp ground.

After marching from Grey Town with the 24th the boys had been placed regularly on the roll of the army, as conductors, and, although they drew no pay, had now the advantage of receiving rations as white men. They had upon the line of march frequently chatted with the young officers of the regiment, who, finding that they were the sons of well-to-do farmers and were cheery, high-spirited lads, took to them very much, and invited them of an evening to join them round the camp-fire.

The last day came, and still no messenger arrived from Cetewayo, and in the evening orders were issued that the column should at daybreak pass the drift and advance into the enemy's country. The troops laid down that night in high spirits, little dreaming of the disaster which was to befall them in the campaign which they thought of so lightly.

CHAPTER V.

ISANDULA.

AT two o'clock on the morning of the 11th of January the bugle sounded the reveillé, and the troops prepared to cross the Buffalo. Tents were struck, baggage piled on the waggons, and the regiments stood to arms at half-past four. The native contingent crossed first. The cavalry brigade under Lieut.-Col. Russell placed their ammunition on a pontoon and rode over. The river was in some places up to the necks of the infantry, and even the cavalry were nearly swept away. The first and second battalions of the 24th crossed on the pontoons. The third regiment of the native contingent threw out skirmishers, but could find no trace of the enemy.

A heavy storm had come on at daybreak, but this left off at nine o'clock. Lieut.-Col. Buller, commanding the Frontier Light Horse, now rode in from the camp of Colonel Wood's force, which had crossed the Blood River and had encamped in Zululand at a spot about thirty-two miles distant. Lord Chelmsford rode over there with an escort of the Natal Mounted Police and the Natal Carabineers, who on their return captured three hundred head of cattle, several horses, and a number of sheep and goats. During the day the waggons, oxen, and ambulances were brought across the river on the platoon.

Early next morning the 1st battalion of the 1st Native Regiment, four companies of the 1st battalion of the 24th, and 300 of the irregular horse started on a reconnaissance towards the kraal of Sirayo, the chief whose sons had been the greatest offenders in the raids into Natal. The cavalry were thrown out in skirmishing order, and after marching nine miles they descended into the slope of the valley in which Sirayo's kraals were situated. The enemy were heard singing their war-songs in one of the ravines, and the 3rd Native Regiment advanced against them with the 24th in reserve. The Zulus opened fire as they approached, and so heavy was this that many of our natives turned and ran ; they were rallied, however, and with a rush carried the caves in which the Zulus were lurking.

In the meantime the 24th's men had moved round to the head of the ravine, and cut off the enemy's retreat. There was a skirmish between the cavalry and some mounted Zulus, and six of these, including a son of Sirayo, were killed. Thirty horses and 400 head of cattle were captured.

The next day was spent in cleaning up arms and accoutrements, after the heavy rain which had fallen the preceding week, and several days were spent in making the roads passable for the waggons.

On the 20th the force moved forward, leaving one company of the 2nd battalion of the 24th, under

Lieutenant Bromhead, with some engineers and a few natives to guard the ford and look after the platoons, and garrison the store and hospital. The column camped at Isandula, or, as it is more properly called, Isandwhlana, ten miles distant from Rorke's Drift. A portion of the road was extremely rough, and the waggons had the greatest difficulty in making their way forward.

The spot selected for a camping-ground was a wide flat valley, with hills on the left and undulating ground on the right; almost in the centre rose an isolated hill, perpendicular on three sides, and very steep and difficult on the fourth. The camp was pitched in front of this hill, looking down the valley, with a mile of open country between it and the hills on the left.

The camp was formed in the following order: on the left were the two battalions of the 3rd Native Regiment; the Royal Artillery were in the centre; next to these was the 2nd battalion of the 24th. The line was then taken up by the cavalry, with the 1st battalion of the 24th on the right of the whole. The waggons were all placed between the camp and the hill at the back.

By a strange and criminal neglect no attempt was made to intrench this position, although it was known that the column might at any moment be attacked by the Zulus.

It was determined that the greater part of the force should advance the next morning towards a stronghold, ten miles distant from the camp, straight

down the valley. News had come that a large number
of Zulus were at this spot, and it was supposed
that these would fight. The column consisted of
eight companies of each of the battalions of the 3rd
Native Regiment, with the greater part of the cavalry.

The force started early and marched for three hours
down the valley. Here they came on much cultivated ground, but the kraals had been deserted by
the enemy. At four o'clock, as the cavalry were
skirmishing at a distance on both flanks, they came
upon a body of Zulus about 2000 strong. The horse
fell back upon the infantry, but, as it was now late,
Major Dartnell decided to encamp for the night, and
to attack in the morning. A messenger was despatched
into camp with a report of the day's proceedings, and
some provisions and blankets were sent out, with news
that the general would join the troops with reinforcements in the morning.

At daybreak he left the camp at Isandula with
seven companies of the 2nd battalion of the 24th,
and orders were sent to Colonel Durnford, at Rorke's
Drift, to bring up 200 mounted men and his rocket-
battery, which had reached that spot.

The Zulus were seen in all directions, and a good
deal of skirmishing took place. By a gross neglect,
equal to that which was manifested in the omission to
fortify the camp, no steps whatever were taken to
keep up communication between the column, which
now consisted of the greater part of the troops, and
those who remained at the camp at Isandula. No

signallers were placed on the hills, no mounted videttes were posted, and the column marched on, absorbed in its own skirmishes with the enemy, as if the general in command had forgotten the very existence of the force at Isandula. Even in the middle of the day, when the firing of cannon told that the camp was attacked, no steps were taken to ascertain whether reinforcements were needed there, and it was not until hours after all was over that a party was despatched to ascertain what had taken place at the camp.

Upon the day on which the two native regiments advanced, the two boys felt the time hang heavy on their hands; they would have liked to take their guns and go out to shoot some game for their dinners, but all shooting had been strictly forbidden, as the sound of a gun might cause a false alarm. After hanging about the camp for an hour or two, Dick proposed that they should climb the hill which rose so steeply behind them.

" If the columns have any fighting," he said, " we should be sure to see it from the top."

Borrowing a telescope from one of the officers of the volunteer cavalry, they skirted round to the back of the hill, and there began their climb. It was very steep, but after some hard work they reached the summit, and then crossed to the front and sat down in a comfortable niche in the rock, whence they could command a view far down the valley. They could see the two battalions of infantry marching steadily along, and the cavalry moving among the hills and undulations on both flanks. They had taken some biscuits and a bottle of beer up with them, and spent the whole day on the look-out. The view which they gained was a very extensive one, as the hill was far higher than those on either side, and in many places they could see small bodies of the enemy moving about. At sunset they descended.

"I vote we go up again," Tom said the next morning. "The general has gone forward with most of the white troops, and there is sure to be fighting to-day. We shall have nothing to do, and may as well go up there as anywhere else."

After the general's departure there remained in camp five companies of the 1st battalion of the 24th, and one of the 2nd battalion, two field-pieces with their artillery-men, and some mounted men.

Just as the boys were starting at eight in the morning, there was a report in the camp that the Zulus were gathering in force to the north of the camp. This quickened the boys' movements and half an hour later they gained the top of the hill, and from their old position looked down upon the camp lying many hundred feet below them. There was considerable bustle going on, and the Kaffir drivers were hastily collecting the cattle which were grazing round, and were driving them into camp.

"There is going to be a fight!" Dick exclaimed, as they gained their look-out; "there are crowds of Zulus out there on the plains."

Could the boys have looked over the hills a mile away to their right, they would have seen that the number of Zulus down in the valley in front was but a small proportion of those gathering for the attack ; for 15,000 men had moved up during the night, and were lying quietly behind those hills, 3000 or 4000 more were taking the road to Rorke's Drift, to cut off any who might escape from the camp, while as many more were showing down the valley. Altogether some 24,000 of the enemy had gathered round the little body in the camp. To the boys, however, only the party down the valley was visible.

At eleven o'clock Colonel Durnford came into camp with his 350 mounted men from Rorke's Drift, and advanced with them to meet the enemy threatening the left flank, while two companies of the 1st battalion of the 24th moved out to attack their right. The Zulus, now reinforced from behind the hills, moved forward steadily, and Colonel Durnford with his cavalry could do little to arrest them. For an hour the infantry stood their ground, and the two field-pieces swept lines through the thick ranks of the enemy. The Zulus advanced in the form of a great crescent.

" Things look very bad, Dick," Tom said ; " what do you think we had better do ? "

" I think we had better stay where we are, Tom, and wait and see what occurs ; we have a splendid view of the fight, and if our fellows meet them we shall see it all ; but if—oh, look there, Tom ! "

Over the hills on the left thousands of Zulus were seen pouring down.

"This is terrible, Tom. Look here, I will crawl

along over the crest, so as not to be seen, and look behind to see if it is clear there. If it is, I vote we make a bolt. It is of no use our thinking of going down for a couple of horses; the Zulus will be in the camp long before we could get there."

Five minutes later he again joined his friend.

"They are coming up behind too, Tom. They have really surrounded us. Look, they are close to the camp!"

It was a scene of frightful confusion. Nothing could be seen of the companies of the 24th, which had gone out to meet the Zulus. The great wave of the advancing army had swept over them. Below, the panic was complete and terrible, and soldiers, native drivers, and camp-followers were running wildly in all directions.

One party of the 24th's men, about sixty strong, had gathered together and stood like a little island. The incessant fire of their rifles covered them with white smoke, while a dense mass of Zulus pressed upon them. Many of the soldiers were flying for their lives; others again, when they found that their retreat was cut off, had gathered in groups and were fighting desperately to the last. Here and there mounted men strove to cut their way through the Zulus, while numbers of fugitives could be seen making for the river, hotly pursued by crowds of the enemy, who speared them as they ran.

"It is frightful, frightful, Tom! I cannot bear to look at it."

For a few minutes the fight continued.   The crack
of the rifles was heard less frequently now.   The
exulting yell of the Zulus rose louder and louder.
On the right Colonel Durnford with his cavalry
essayed to make one last stand to check the pursuit
of the Zulus and give time for the fugitives to escape ;
but it was in vain, showers of assegais fell among
them, and the Zulu crowd surged round.

For a time the boys thought all were lost, but a
few horsemen cut their way through the crowd and
rode for the river.   The artillery had long before
ceased to fire, and the gunners lay speared by the
cannons.   The first shot had been fired at half-past
eleven, by one o'clock all was over.   The last
white man had fallen, and the Zulus swarmed like
a vast body of ants over the camp in search of
plunder.

Horror-stricken and sick, the boys shrank back
against the rock behind them, and for some time
sobbed bitterly over the dreadful massacre which had
taken place before their eyes.   But after a time they
began to talk more quietly.

"Will they come up here, do you think, Dick?"

"No, I don't think so," Dick replied.   "They could
hardly have seen us come up here, even if they had
been on the look-out on the hills, and as they reached
the back of the mountain before the camp was taken,
they will know that nobody could have come up afterwards.   Lie back here; we cannot possibly be seen from
below. They will be too much taken up with plundering

the camp to think of searching this hill. What on earth is the general doing ?—I can see his troops right away on the plain. Surely he must have heard the guns ? Our only hope now is that when he hears it he will march straight back ; but, even if he does, I fear that the Zulus will be too strong for him. The whole force which he has with him is no stronger than that which has been crushed here, and I don't expect the native regiments can make much stand if attacked by such a tremendously strong force."

So long as the daylight lasted, the boys, peering occasionally over, could see the Zulus at the work of plundering. All the sacks and barrels were taken from the waggons and cut or broken open, each man taking as much as he could carry of the tea, sugar, flour, and other necessaries ; many of the yoke-oxen were assegaied at once, and cut up and eaten, the rest being driven off towards the north by a party of warriors.

At nightfall the tents were set on fire; they soon burnt out, and the boys could no longer see what was taking place. Rising from the shelter, they walked back to the other side of the crest.

" I can hear firing now," Dick said ; " it seems to me that it is back at Rorke's Drift."

They were soon sure that they were not mistaken ; as it grew darker a flittering light was seen in that direction, and a continued fire of distant musketry was heard. Later on there was a broad glare in the sky.

"I fear it is all over there too," Dick said, "and that the place has been burnt."

Still, however, the firing continued, as heavy as ever, and long on into the night the lads sat listening to it. At last they fell asleep, and when they awoke the sun was already high. Thus they missed their chance of escape.

At nine o'clock in the evening Lord Chelmsford's force, hearing at last what had happened, marched back into the camp, and before day had fairly broken continued their way down to Rorke's Drift. The defenders here, a little garrison, under Lieutenant Bromhead of the 24th, and Chard of the Royal Artillery, had made an heroic defence against some 4000 of the enemy. With mealy bags and boxes they built up a breastwork, and this they held all night, in spite of the desperate efforts of the Zulus to capture it. The hospital, which stood at one end of the intrenchment, was carried and burnt by the Zulus, but the little garrison held out till morning in an inner intrenchment round the store-house.

Here was seen what could be done in the way of defence by the aid of hastily-thrown-up intrenchments; and had breastworks been erected at Isandula, as they ought to have been the instant the troops arrived there, and still more so when the major portion of the column marched away, the force there, small as it was, would doubtless have made a successful resistance. Even had the step been taken, when the Zulus were first seen approaching, of forming a laager—that is, of drawing up the waggons in the form of a hollow square—at the foot of the steep mountain, the disaster might have been averted. It may be said that the massacre of Isandula was due entirely to the over-confidence and carelessness of the officers in command of the column.

The boys on waking crawled back cautiously to a spot where they could obtain a view over the valley, and, to their surprise, the force which, on the afternoon before, they had seen out there had entirely disappeared. Many bodies of Zulus were seen moving about, but there was no trace of the white troops. They made their way to the back of the hill, and then, to their horror, saw the column moving away from them, and already half-way on its road to Rorke's Drift.

Their first impulse was to get up and start off in a run in pursuit of it, but this feeling lasted but a moment, for between the hill and the column many scattered parties of Zulus were to be seen. The boys looked blankly at each other. It was but too clear that they were cut off and alone in the enemy's country.

"Whatever shall we do, Dick?"

"I have not the least idea, Tom. At any rate there is nothing to be done at present. We should be assegaied in a moment if we were to go down; let's go back to our old look-out."

After much talk they agreed that it would be hopeless to attempt to make south and cross the Buffalo, as many of the fugitives had done. There were sure

to be strong bodies of Zulus along the river, and even
if they passed these without detection they would be
unable to cross the river, as they would find no ford,
and neither of them was able to swim.

There were great numbers of Zulus in the camp
below, and these seemed to be pursuing the work of
plundering more minutely than they had done on the
previous day. The stores scattered recklessly about
were collected, placed in empty barrels, and loaded
up on the waggons. Presently a number of cattle
were brought down ; these were harnessed to the
waggons and driven off, and by nightfall nothing save
scattered remnants marked the place where the British
camp had stood. But from their post the boys could
see that the ground far and near was dotted with
corpses, black and white.

After nightfall the boys descended to the camp, and
having marked the exact spot where the waggons had
stood were able to collect a number of pieces of the
broken biscuit scattered about ; they were fortunate
enough to light upon a water-bottle still full, and with
these treasures they returned to the post on the mountain. They had agreed to wait there for three or four
days, in fact as long as they could hold out, and then
quietly to walk into one of the native kraals. If
caught in the act of flight they were certain of being
killed, but they hoped that when the Zulus' blood had
cooled down after the conflict their lives might possibly
be spared.

This plan was carried out ; for four days they

remained on the hill of Isandula, and then descending late one evening to the plain walked for ten or twelve miles north, and waiting until daybreak showed them a large native kraal at no great distance, they made for it, and sat quietly down at the door of the principal hut. Presently a girl issued from a neighbouring hut, and, upon seeing them, gave a scream and ran back again. The cry brought others to the doors of the huts. When the boys were seen, a perfect hubbub of tongues broke forth, and many of the men, running out with their spears, advanced towards the lads. They sat perfectly quiet, and held up their hands to show that they were unarmed. The Zulus hesitated. Dick went through the motion of eating and drinking, and in his best Kaffir begged for a glass of water.

The Zulus, seeing that the boys were alone, approached them, and began to ask them questions, and were evidently much surprised at hearing that they had escaped from the massacre of the British. From the door of the hut in which they were sitting a chief, evidently of high rank, for the others greeted him respectfully, now came out.

After the cause of the tumult was explained to the chief, he ordered the boys to be bound. This was done and they were put into an empty hut while their fate was decided upon ; after much deliberation it was agreed by the Zulus that, as they were but boys and had come into the camp unarmed and of their own accord, their lives should for the present be spared.

It happened that in the village were a party of men who belonged to the tribe of Umbelleni, whose territory lay to the north-west, and these volunteered to take the prisoners to their chief, who was one of the strongest opponents of the English. His country, indeed, lay just within the Zulu frontier, and, having been engaged in constant skirmishes and broils with the Dutch settlers, he was even more disappointed than the other chiefs at the taking over of the Transvaal by England, just at the time when the Zulus were meditating its conquest.

The road from Itelezi, the village at which the boys had given themselves up, to Umbelleni's country ran along between the Blood River and the lofty hill-country; and, although they were ignorant of the fact, Colonel Wood's force was at that moment lying on this line. They were therefore taken up over a mountain-country, crossing Mount Ingwe, to the Zlobani Mountain, a stronghold ten miles south of Umbelleni's chief kraal, and where at present he was residing. After three days' journey the lads, exhausted and footsore, ascended to the plateau of the Zlobani Mountains.

Upon their way they passed through many villages, and at each place it needed the efforts of their guards to prevent their being seriously maltreated, if not killed. The Zulus, although victorious at Isandula, had suffered terribly, it being estimated that nearly 3000 had fallen in the attack.

Thus there was not a village but had lost some of

its members, for, although the Zulu regiments have iocal denominations and regular military kraals, each regiment consists of men drawn from the population at large.

Every four or five years all the lads who have passed the age of eighteen since the formation of the last corps, are called out and formed into a regiment, or are embodied with some regiment whose numbers have fallen in strength. Thus a regiment may consist of men differing considerably from each other in point of age, the great distinction being that some corps consist entirely of married men, while others are all unmarried. A regiment remains unmarried until the king formally gives the permission to take wives, and the corps to whom the boon has been granted are distinguished from the others by their hair being arranged in a thick ring round the head. So great is the enmity between these married regiments and their less fortunate comrades that they are never encamped in each other's view, as fighting in that case would inevitably take place. Thus it happened that, although some of the corps had suffered far more than others, the loss was spread over the whole of Zululand.

CHAPTER VI.

ZLOBANI.

WHILE disaster had fallen upon the centre column, the division under Colonel Evelyn Wood had been showing what could be done when care and prudence took the place of a happy-go-lucky recklessness. It had advanced from Utrecht on the 7th of January, and had moved up to the frontier at Sandspruit. At two in the afternoon of the 10th it moved forward, halted at six, and again advanced by the light of the moon at half-past one in the morning; a mounted advance-guard was thrown out, flanking patrols were organized, and the troops moved in the greatest silence.

The next day Colonel Buller, with his irregular horse, went out, and after a skirmish with the Zulus brought in a thousand cattle, and Captain Barton, with a party scouting in another direction, captured 550.

On the following morning a reconnaissance in force was made, and a good deal of skirmishing took place; but, as Colonel Wood never allowed his men to follow the Zulus into rough ground, the latter were unable to effect anything against the column. This division advanced forward but slowly, as it was intended that they should keep within reach of the leisurely-moving central column.

After several slight skirmishes the news reached

them on the 24th of the disaster of Isandula, and with
it Colonel Wood received orders to fall back ; and on
the 26th he encamped at Kambula. Raids were made
in all directions with great success ; the great military
kraal of Manyamyoba was captured and destroyed by
Colonel Buller and his cavalry. As Colonel Wood's
was now the most advanced column, Colonel Rowlands,
with a wing of the 80th and a couple of guns and 200
Swazis, together with Raaf's Horse and Wetherby's
Borderers, were sent as a reinforcement to him.

The Zulus were not idle, and Umbelleni and
Manyamyoba made several successful raids across the
border and destroyed the kraals of natives friendly to
the English. These two chiefs were not regular Zulu
chieftains ; both were adventurers who had gathered
under them numbers of broken men, and had for
years carried on raids on their own account from their
mountain-stronghold, in much the same way that
the Scotch borderers of olden times harassed the
country on the English side of the frontier.

Oham, the king's brother, with his own following,
came into Colonel Wood's camp, and gave himself up,
saying that he was altogether opposed to the war.

The boys on their arrival at Zlobani were brought
before Umbelleni. That chief briefly gave orders
that they should be killed ; but two or three of his
headmen represented to him that they might be of
use ; they would be able to carry a message to the
British camp, should he desire at any time to send
one ; by their appearance and dress, they could tell

him the nature of any troops they might intend to attack, and could read and explain any letters which might be captured on messengers ; finally, they might be an acceptable present to send to Cetewayo, who might not be pleased if he heard that prisoners had been killed in cold blood.

Umbelleni assented to the reasoning, and ordered the boys to be taken to a hut. The Zulu dwellings resemble in form great bee-hives. They are circular and dome-roofed ; the entrance is but three feet high, and people can only enter by crawling. A woman was ordered to cook for them. No guard was placed over them, and they were permitted to wander about freely, as escape from such a position was considered impossible.

Six weeks passed slowly, and on the 11th of March a messenger arrived, and there was a sudden stir in the camp. In a few minutes the fighting men assembled. The boys were ordered to take their place in the column, and at a swift march, with which they had the greatest difficulty in keeping up, the column moved away.

"Where are they taking us now, I wonder?" Tom said.

"I suppose they are going to attack some English party on the march ; our men are hardly likely, I should think, again to be caught napping, as they were at Isandula."

Crossing two rivers, the Bevana and Pongola, they at night halted in another mountain-kraal of Umbelleni, about three miles from the Intombe River. On the bank of the river could be seen twenty waggons. These waggons had come down from Derby, on their way to Luneberg, a town situated four miles from the Intombe. Major Tucker, who commanded there, sent Captain Moriarty with a company of the 80th, seventy strong, down to the river to protect the waggons whilst crossing, and that officer had orders to neglect no precaution, and above all to keep an incessant and vigilant look-out.

The river was in flood, and no crossing could be effected, and for four days the waggons remained on the northern bank. Captain Moriarty placed the waggons in laager on the bank, and took post there with forty of his men, leaving Lieutenant Harwood with thirty-four on the south bank with directions to cover the sides of the laager with a flanking fire, should it be attacked. The position of the waggons was a dangerous one, as the ground rose immediately behind them, and was covered with bush.

In the middle of the night of the 11th Umbelleni's men arose, and, accompanied by the boys, started from the kraal, and Dick and Tom were filled with forebodings of what was about to happen. Dick had already gathered from the natives that the guard of the waggons was an extremely small one, and, as the body moving to attack them were between 4000 and 5000 strong, the chance of a successful resistance appeared small.

When within a short distance of the waggons two of the Zulus motioned to the boys to stop. In ten minutes they heard a sentry challenge ; his shout was answered by a loud yell, and the Zulus poured down to the attack.   Unfortunately Captain Moriarty had not taken sufficient precaution against surprise, and before the men were fairly under arms the Zulus were upon them.

The force on the other side of the river were now on the alert, and their rifle-fire opened before that of the defenders of the waggons.   For a moment or two there was a sharp rattling fire from the waggons ; then there were shouts and screams, the firing ceased, and the boys knew that the laager had been captured. Many of the soldiers indeed were assegaied before they could leave their tents, most were slaughtered at once, but a few managed to swim across the river. The Zulus swarmed after them.   Lieutenant Harwood jumped upon his horse and rode off to Luneberg to fetch assistance.   The little detachment was broken by the rush of the Zulus, but a serjeant and eight men fell back into a deserted kraal, and succeeded in repelling the attacks of the enemy.

Lieutenant Harwood was afterwards tried by court-martial for his conduct ; he was acquitted, but the general in command refused to confirm the verdict, and the commander-in-chief at home approved of the view he took of the matter, and issued a general order to the effect that "An officer, being the only one present with a party of soldiers actually engaged with the enemy, is not under any pretext whatever justified in deserting them, and thus by so doing abandoning them to their fate."

Apprehensive of the arrival of reinforcements from Luneberg, Umbelleni did not continue his attack upon the little party in the kraal, but, after hastily plundering the waggons, retreated with his force, and the next day returned to Zlobani.

A few days passed and the boys learnt that two regiments from Ulundi were expected shortly to reinforce Umbelleni's men. The chief himself, with the majority of his followers, was now at his kraal, four miles distant, but the boys remained in the village on the Zlobani plateau. Several times they saw parties of British horse riding over the plains and from a distance reconnoitring the position, and they wondered whether there could be any intention on the part of Colonel Wood to attack it. There was on the plateau a large number of cattle, part the property of Umbelleni's men, but the great majority spoil taken in raids. It seemed to the boys that an attack could scarcely be successful. The sides of the mountains were extremely precipitous, covered with bush, and contained large numbers of caves. There was but one path up which mounted men could ride; this was about half-way along the west side, the hill being a much greater length from north to south than from east to west. Up the southern extremity of the plateau was a path by which footmen could descend to the plain, but it was exceedingly steep and altogether impracticable for cavalry; a handful of men should have been able to hold the position against an army.

Colonel Wood having heard of the large quantity of cattle concealed on the Zlobani Mountain had determined to attack it, and at three o'clock in the morning of the 27th of March a cavalry party started. It consisted of 150 mounted infantry ; the Frontier Light Horse, 125 ; Raaf's Troop, 50 ; Piet-Uys' Boer Contingent, 50 ; Wetherby's Horse, 80 ; Schermbrucker's Horse, 40 ;—a total of 495 men. They were commanded by Colonel Russell, and Colonel Wood was himself to join them in the evening. The party was a picked one, all being well mounted and good rifle-shots.

The track led across a rough sandy country with deep nullahs, and thickly covered with trees and bush. At five o'clock they halted for half an hour, and then again advanced. After five miles' travelling across a very rough country they came out into a large cultivated flat, which terminated in a long, dark, winding gorge, black with bush and skirted by precipices of sandstone and granite. They turned into this and followed a rivulet until they came to the end of the gorge, where they discovered a steep path which seemed cut out of the solid rock, and was only wide enough for one horseman to pass. After three quarters of an hour's climbing they gained the summit.

The country was wild in the extreme. The plateau upon which they found themselves extended for seven or eight miles. Huge masses of scrub and boulders, peaks, terraces, and ledges of rock appeared everywhere, while caves and immense fissures formed retreats for the cattle. It was now late in the afternoon, and the force bivouacked for the night, having brought with them three days' provisions. At seven in the evening Colonel Wood joined them with his staff, eight mounted men of the 50th regiment and six natives under Untongo, a son of Pongo, a friendly chief. Untongo had by some means obtained information that seven strong regiments had marched from Ulundi seven days before, and was most anxious that the column should return to Kambula.

Colonel Wood, however, could not carry out this advice, for Colonels Buller and Wetherby and Piet-Uys, with their commands, who were in front, had moved forward a long distance, and a retreat now would leave them to be surrounded and cut off. The troops lay down and slept, and at half-past three o'clock again prepared to advance. Distant shots were heard, showing that Colonel Buller was attacked, and just as the party was setting off, Colonel Wetherby with his troopers rode in, having in the night got separated from Buller's men in the wild and broken country. As the troops advanced they came here and there across the bodies of Zulus, showing that Buller had had to fight his way. Captain Ronald Campbell ascended a rock and scanned the country with his glass. Far away, almost in the centre of the gigantic and apparently inaccessible cliff of Zlobani, the remains of Buller's column could be seen slowly advancing, driving some dark masses of cattle and Zulus before them.

Colonel Wetherby obtained permission to lead his men on at once to Buller's assistance, while Colonel Wood followed with the remainder of the force.

Wetherby moved by a terribly difficult path to the right, while Wood kept to what seemed the main track. About half a mile further the latter came on a party of 200 Zulus, armed with rifles ; these crossed in front of him, taking an occasional shot at the leading files of the party, who on account of the difficulties of the road were compelled to dismount and lead their horses. Their object was evidently to cut off Wetherby's troop from the main column. Lieutenant Lysons, leaving the column, reconnoitred the ground, and found that Wetherby's party was already divided from them by a deep and impassable ravine, at the bottom of which was the pathway by which Buller had made his way to the summit of the cliff. A strong party of Zulus were seen far away in front, working as if to cut off Buller's horse. It was clear that there was nothing to do but to press forward in hopes that the line taken by Wetherby and that which the main column was following would come together.

At this moment a heavy fire was opened by a party of the enemy from a narrow ledge of rock a hundred yards above them. Untongo and two of his men guided a party of eight marksmen to a still higher point, and their fire speedily drove off the Zulus. Half an hour's march brought Wood upon Wetherby's track, and high above them to the right the rear of Buller's column could be seen. No more unsuitable ground for the operation of mounted men could be found ; perpendicular rocks rose in all directions, while steep precipices fell away at their feet. Killed and wounded horses were seen at every turn of the road, showing how stoutly the enemy had held their ground, and how difficult an operation Buller had performed. Sending fifty men to work upon the right flank and endeavour to take the Zulus in the rear, Colonel Wood kept his men for a few moments under cover of a friendly ledge of rocks, to take breath and look to their rifles, girths, and ammunition, and then pressed rapidly forward and joined the Border Horse.

The scene was now most exciting. The firing was almost continuous, and the yells of the savages rose from every rock and bush, mingled with the loud cheers of Buller's men far up in front, as they saw the column approaching to their aid. The ground was now more level and practicable for riding, and Colonel Wood mounted his horse and, accompanied by his own little escort of a dozen men and the Border Horse under Colonel Wetherby himself, with his gallant boy, aged fifteen, who was fighting by his side, galloped forward for the front, leaving Colonel Russell in command of the column. When within a hundred paces of the summit of the cliff a rain of fire opened upon their front and flank from a mass of Zulus firing from caves, crevices, and behind enormous boulders. From one cave to the right front an excessively heavy fire was kept up, and Colonel Wetherby dashed at this with his men just as Colonel Wood's horse staggered from a deep assegai wound in the chest. At the same moment a native from behind a boulder fired at that officer at ten paces' distance; the bullet missed him and Lieutenant Lloyd rode at the man, but fell, shot through the head. Colonel Wood and Captain Ronald Campbell rode forward to cover his body. Two more Zulus fired at the same instant and the colonel's horse fell dead. Colonel Wetherby's men were hotly engaged at close quarters with the Zulus, and were unable to join the colonel. Captain Campbell, Lieutenant Lysons, and the eight 90th men of the escort rushed at the opening. Captain Campbell fell, shot through the head, but the rest dashed forward.

There was a movement in the cave and a sudden shout in English of " Come on !" and as the little band dashed in and fell upon the Zulus they saw, to their astonishment, two English boys, armed with assegais, attacking these in the rear. In another minute the Zulus were all cut down, and the party returned to Colonel Wood.

On the previous afternoon Zulu scouts had arrived at Zlobani with the news that an English column was on its way towards it. Messengers were despatched to Umbelleni's kraal, and at night his force there came to the assistance of those at Zlobani. Early in the morning the boys proceeded with a number of Zulus to the edge of the plateau, and were placed with eight of their guards in a cave. From its mouth they watched anxiously the events of the day.

Colonel Buller's party had struck upon the right road, and after hard fighting gained the summit of the cliff. Here a great quantity of cattle were collected, and these were sent off in charge of a body of friendly natives, which accompanied the force. This column in the advance had not passed near the cave in which the boys were placed. Their hearts beat high as they saw Colonel Wood's column suddenly turn off from the line which Buller had followed, and make straight for it. Their excitement grew higher and higher as the conflict increased in vigour.

Soon the Zulus in the cave were at work. When Captain Campbell charged forward with his handful of men, Dick and Tom exchanged a glance. They stood quiet until it was evident that the English attack would be pushed home; then, as the men of the 90th, led by Lysons, dashed at the entrance of the cavern, the boys seized two assegais and each pinned one of the crouching Zulus to the ground. Before the others could turn round upon them Lysons and his men were among them.

The fire of Buller's men from above drove the Zulus from their hiding-places. But Colonel Wood, finding it impossible to make his way up at this point, moved round at the foot of the rocks, to try and find the point at which Buller had ascended the cliff. Before doing so, however, the bodies of Captain Campbell and Lieutenant Lloyd were carried down the hill, and buried in a hastily-made grave. As, carrying their wounded men, the little party made their way to the foot of the cliff, Untongo, who had been reconnoitring the rocks on both sides, ran down to him and began to talk rapidly, pointing over towards the plain.

Colonel Wood did not understand Kaffir, but Dick, who was standing by, said,—

" He says, sir, that there is a great Zulu army marching below."

Colonel Wood mounted a fresh horse, and making his way with great difficulty across some broken ground reached a point where he could see the plain. There, in five continuous columns, the Zulu army from Ulundi, 20,000 strong, was sweeping along at its usual rapid pace. It was evident at once that only by a speedy retreat could any of the force hope to escape. Colonel Wood despatched a message at once to Colonel Russell, who had with his force by this time commenced the ascent at the extreme westerly point, to retrace his steps instantly, and to cover as far as possible the retreat of the native allies with the cattle.

Colonel Buller above had also seen the coming danger. So far he had accomplished his work admirably. The Zulu position had been triumphantly stormed, and a large number of cattle taken and driven off.

Had Colonel Wood's force and Wetherby's troop arrived on the scene of action immediately after Buller had ascended to the plateau, the retreat could have been made in time, and the expedition would have been successful at all points. The unfortunate incident of their losing the track, the delay caused thereby, and their inability to rejoin him had given time for the Ulundi army to come up.

Colonel Buller found that it was impossible now to descend to the plain by the path by which he had ascended. Not only would he have to fight his way back through the whole force of Umbelleni, but his retreat by that route would be cut off by the Ulundi men. Consequently, pursued by a great body of exulting Zulus, he made his way along the plateau to the steep path at its extremity.

The scene here was terrible. The Zulus blocked the way in front and lined both sides. Buller himself, with Piet-Uys, defended the rear, assisting the wounded, and often charging desperately into the ranks of the Zulus pressing upon him. The path was slippery with blood and strewn with dead. As the last of his troop made their way down it, Piet-Uys, a most gallant Dutchman, fell dead across the body of his horse, with six Zulus, whom he had shot with his revolver, around him.

Wetherby's troop was surrounded, and forty-five out of his eighty men killed. The colonel himself and his boy both fell, the latter refusing to leave his father, although the latter urged him to gallop off and join the column, which appeared to be making its way through the Zulus. Colonel Russell's command got through without so much opposition ; but Buller's horse, Piet-Uys' troop, and Wetherby's command suffered terribly.

Fortunately the Ulundi army did not follow the retreat; first, because the tremendous three days' march which they had made had in a great measure exhausted the men, who had started in such haste that they had brought no provisions with them, and secondly, on account of the steady attitude and resolute bearing of Russell's command.

Buller's force reached Kambula camp at half-past seven at night. It had set in stormy, and torrents of rain were falling. Although he had been in the saddle for forty-eight hours, Colonel Buller, on hearing that a small party of the survivors had taken refuge in hiding ten miles away, collected a party of volunteers, and, taking led horses, set out to rescue them. This was effected; the fugitives were found to be seven in number, and returned with their rescuers safely to camp.

The boys had both escaped, two of Wetherby's men, who accompanied Colonel Wood, taking them on their saddles behind them. The total loss was ten officers and seventy-eight men.

For the night the boys were handed over to the charge of one of the officers of the staff, but in the morning Colonel Wood sent for them, and they then told him the story of their adventures since the battle of Isandula, with which he was greatly interested. He said that he would at once have sent them to Utrecht, but that the camp would probably be attacked during the day.

The troops had been on the alert all night, expecting an attack. Before daylight Captain Raaf was sent out with twenty-five men to reconnoitre, and returned with one of Oham's natives. This man had joined the Zulu army as it advanced, and was, fortunately for himself, not recognized by them as being one of Oham's people. In the night he had slipped away. He reported the Zulus 20,000 strong, a great portion of them being armed with rifles.

Fortunately little preparation was necessary at Kambula. Nothing had been left to chance here, and there was therefore no fear of a repetition of the Isandula disaster. Each corps, each subdivision, each section, and each man had his place allotted to him, and had been told to be in that place at the sound of the bugle.

The little fort was in a strong position, laid out upon an elevated narrow reach of table-land. A precipice, inaccessible to a white man, guarded the right flank ; on the left a succession of steep terraces had been utilized and carefully intrenched, each successive line commanding that below it. At one end there was a narrow slip of land swept by two 7-pounders. Immediately in the rear, upon an eminence 120 feet higher than the fort, was a small work, armed with two guns. The camp consisted of an outer defence of 100 waggons, and an inner one of fifty—the whole protected by earthworks and ditches.

CHAPTER VII.

KAMBULA.

IMMEDIATELY Oham's Zulu had made his report, the bugle sounded, and the garrison quietly and quickly took up the places assigned to them. Messengers went out to order a fatigue-party, which had gone out wood-cutting, to return at once. These men reported that they had seen the Zulus scouting, about five miles to the west. The tents were struck, the men lined the shelter-trenches, and ammunition was served out by fatigue-parties told off for this duty. The white conductors and commissariat men, most of whom were old settlers and good shots, were told off to the different faces of the laager. A small party were provided with stretchers, in order to carry the wounded to the hospital in the centre.

Dick and Tom, having no duty and being without arms, thought that they might as well make themselves useful at this work, and therefore, taking a stretcher, they proceeded to one of the outer shelter-trenches.

It was nearly eleven o'clock when the Zulus were seen approaching, and halted just out of musket-range. Here apparently a council of war was held, and it was more than an hour before any forward movement was made. Then a body of them, about 7000 strong, ran at a tremendous pace along a ledge situated at the edge of the cultivated land. The troops were ordered not to fire, as it was thought better to wait until the Zulus came on in earnest. At half-past one a cloud of skirmishers advanced from the Zulu army, and fed by supports began to scale the north front of the English position. Here, behind the outermost line of intrenchments, some of Buller and Russell's dismounted men, and a portion of the band of the gallant Piet-Uys were stationed, and these opened fire upon the Zulus. Scarcely one of them but was a dead-shot, and no sooner did a head or a shield appear above rock or boulder or tuft of grass than the deadly rifle rang out, and in most cases there was an enemy the less to encounter.

The Boers particularly distinguished themselves at this work. Most of these men are certain shots, being trained from childhood in the use of their large single-barrelled guns, carrying an enormous bullet, and suited for the destruction of big game. Animated by a hatred of the Zulus, and a longing for vengeance for the death of their late leader, the Boers picked off their foes with unerring aim. The enemy's skirmishers now retired, and a more solid line took their place, supported by a dense column in its rear. The cavalry remounted and fell slowly back, and Major Russell, with twenty of his men, made a brilliant charge on a party of Zulus who were running to take possession of a sheltering ledge of rocks, and, after cutting down a great many, retreated without the loss of a man.

Buller and Russell now retired slowly within the laager, their retreat being covered by Colonel Gilbert and four companies of the 13th, who were posted at this face of the works. One company of the 13th, under Captain Cox, held the cattle-laager, which was situated outside the line, and so were able to take the enemy in flank, as they attacked the main work. This little garrison and Colonel Gilbert's men poured a tremendous fire upon the Zulus, who still, however, pushed forward.

Major Hackett was now ordered to take a couple of companies of the 90th, and to advance up the slope, round the rear of the cattle-laager. Taking post here, they opened a deliberate and deadly fire upon the enemy, and then advancing drove back the Zulus with great loss. The Zulu general, however, led a party of his best marksmen round to his right, and opened a heavy fire upon the 90th, as they fell back upon their intrenchments. Lieutenant Bright fell mortally wounded, and in running forward to pick him up Major Hackett was struck by a ball sideways, which passed through both eyes and destroyed his sight for ever. Meanwhile, from the works on the heights, Captain Nicholson was doing great execution with his two 7-pounders. The Zulu main body had now come within range, and grape and canister were poured into their heavy masses. As Nicholson was standing on the parapet, field-glass in hand. directing the pointing of two guns, a bullet struck him on the temple and he fell dead. He was seen from the laager to fall, and Major Vaughan was sent to take his place. Major Tremlett, R.A., now took the four guns, hitherto held in reserve, to a small piece of rising ground outside the laager, and opened fire upon the masses of the enemy with immense execution. From time to time Buller and Russell, as they saw openings for a charge, swept down and drove the enemy's skirmishers back on to their main body; the Zulus, altogether unaccustomed to cavalry, always falling back precipitately at these assaults.

At three o'clock a hot cross-fire was opened upon a company commanded by Captain Woodgate, which was stationed half-way between the laager and the upper fort, keeping open a communication between them, the enemy's fire from a height commanding this line being particularly galling. Two of Tremlett's guns were brought to bear on the point, and the enemy's fire speedily slackened. For another hour and a half the troops continued to be hotly engaged, for the enemy, when driven back from one flank, swept round in most perfect order and attacked another.

At half-past four the Zulus, concentrating again, attacked the northern side, and made some desperate rushes up to the muzzles of the English rifles, and the fighting for a time was almost hand to hand.

The boys had worked round with their stretchers wherever the fire was hardest, and had carried many wounded men into hospital. They were at the north face when the Zulus swarmed up towards it, and Woodgate's men fell back into the shelter of the laager. As they came in, a young lieutenant, who was commanding the rear, fell, apparently dead. Being in the rear of the company his fall was unnoticed by the men. Dick, who was peering over the intrenchment, saw him fall, and saw too that he moved slightly.

"Quick, Tom!" he exclaimed; and, carrying the stretcher, the boys scrambled over the breastwork and ran towards the officer. He had fallen some twenty yards outside, and the Zulus, rushing on, were but eighty yards away.

On reaching the side of the young officer, the boys laid their stretcher on the ground, rolled him upon it, and, lifting it, turned towards the camp. A ringing cheer from the men had greeted this action, mingled with shouts of "Run! run!" for by this time the Zulus were but twenty yards behind.

A stream of fire broke out from the top of the breastworks; an assegai whizzed over Dick's shoulder, and another grazed Tom's arm, but they hurried on until they reached the ditch, and then threw themselves and their burden down. There for five or six minutes they lay, while the fight raged above them. Then the British cheer rose, and the boys knew that the Zulus had fallen back.

A minute later a dozen men leapt from the intrenchment into the ditch outside, and lifted the wounded lieutenant over it into the arms of those behind.

TOM AND DICK HURRY FORWARD TO RESCUE THE
WOUNDED OFFICER.

"Bravo! boys, bravo!" a hundred voices shouted, as the boys scrambled back into the works, while the men crowded round to pat them on the shoulder and shake their hands.

It was evident now that the Zulu fire was slackening, and three companies of the 13th went out, and, taking posts by the edge of the slope of the cattle-laager, opened fire upon them, as they retired. Every gun was brought to bear upon them, and as, disheartened and beaten, they fell back, Buller and Russell, with every mounted man in camp, sallied out and fell upon them, and, burning with the desire to wipe out their misfortune of the preceding day, chased them for seven miles, like a flock of sheep, cutting down immense numbers.

It was ascertained afterwards from prisoners that the Zulu force which attacked was composed of 25,000 men. It was commanded by Tyangwaiyo, with Umbelleni as his second. Many of the leading chiefs of Zululand and 3000 of the king's bravest and best troops fell in the attack on Kambula, and this battle was by far the hottest and best-contested which took place during the war.

Upon our side two officers and twenty-one men were killed. The difference between the result of the action at Kambula and that at Isandula was due entirely to the fact that in one case every precaution was taken, every means of defence utilized; while in the other no more attention was paid to any of these points than if the troops had been encamped at Aldershot.

Upon the day following the battle Colonel Wood set his men to work to erect further defences at the points which the recent action had shown to be weak, and never ceased work until the place had been made almost impregnable against an assault of savages, however brave.

The messenger who carried to Natal the news of the victory of Kambula also took letters from the boys to their parents, acquainting them of their safety; and with the first convoy of wounded on the following day the boys started for home, Colonel Wood having given to each a flattering testimonial as to their gallant conduct in the action, and having presented them with two horses belonging to men of Buller's corps who had fallen in the action, ordering that the horses should be entered as bought for the Queen's service, and the value paid to the relatives of their late owners.

Three days' march took the convoy to Utrecht, and the next morning the boys rode home, the distance from there to Newcastle being about forty miles. They were received as if they had risen from the dead, for their letters had not arrived before them, and their parents had of course assumed that they had been killed at Isandula. Both the mothers were in mourning, and their joy at the restoration of their sons was unbounded.

Mrs. Jackson fainted from surprise and delight, as Tom rode up ; but Dick, remembering the effect which the news of his being alive in the snow had produced upon his mother, was careful to save her the shock. Accordingly, instead of riding direct to the house, he made a détour and rode across the farm until he met Bill Harrison. The man was delighted at the sight of his young master, and could hardly believe his eyes, as he saw him riding towards him.

After the first warm greeting was over, Dick learned that his mother had been seriously ill, and was now recovering, and that his father had been much shaken. Dick told Harrison to go to the house, and, under the excuse of some question about his work, to call Mr. Humphreys out, and to tell him of his return, leaving it to him to break the news to his wife.

This Mr. Humphreys, after recovering from his own emotion at the joyful intelligence, did so gradually and quietly, that the tale produced no injurious effect upon the mother.

He began by saying that he had heard that a rumour was afloat that some of those that were supposed to have been killed at Isandula had been kept captives by the Zulus.

Mrs. Humphreys for a time doubted the news, but, upon her husband's assurance that the intelligence was well founded, a faint feeling of hope began to spring up; then gradually, step by step, he told her that it was reported that these captives consisted chiefly of non-combatants, men who had taken refuge among the rocks and bushes when the fight was seen to be going against the troops. This still further raised Mrs. Humphreys' hopes; for, from the presence of mind and shrewdness which Dick had shown on the occasion of the snow-storm, it seemed probable that he would be quick to avail himself of any chance of escape there might be. Then Mr. Humphreys said that the report affirmed that among the prisoners were two or three quite young lads, and so step by step he went on, until the delighted mother learned that her son was already upon the farm, and was only waiting until he knew she would be strong enough to see him.

Mr. Humphreys now went to the door and gave a loud shout, and Dick, who had been waiting the signal agreed on at a short distance from the house, ran up and was soon in his parents' arms. A minute or two later his younger brother ran in, having just heard the news from Harrison, and it was indeed a happy party which that night assembled in the sitting-room of the farmhouse, and listened to Dick's account of the adventures he had gone through. Not a little proud were the father and mother, as they read Colonel Wood's testimony to the gallant conduct of their son.

The next day Mr. and Mrs. Jackson drove over with Tom, and the warmest congratulations were exchanged.

"Have you been paid for the waggons, father?" Dick asked.

"Yes, my boy, for there was a notice that the owners of all waggons and teams destroyed at Isandula would be paid at once. As there was a record kept of the ownership of those which accompanied the column, there was of course no difficulty in proving the loss, and both Mr. Jackson and myself received orders on the public treasury for their value last week. You see more transports were required, and there was such a panic after Isandula, that if government had not promptly paid for their losses there, they would have got no more waggons from farmers for their work. We have already four more building for us at Newcastle."

"I suppose there was a great fright in the colony after the defeat?"

"Terrible!" Mr. Humphreys answered. "Every one imagined that the Zulus would at once cross the frontier, and carry fire and sword throughout the colony. The rest of the 4th Regiment instantly went forward to Colonel Glyn's column, and this restored it to something like its strength before the fight. The rivers were high, which may have accounted partly for the Zulus not taking the offensive. Probably too the great loss which they themselves must have suffered had some effect ; while they might not have liked to have advanced in force across the frontier, being, as they were, threatened on the one side by the column of Colonel Wood at Kambula, and on the other by that of Colonel Pearson at Ekowe."

"I have not heard about that column, father. What are they doing?"

"I will tell you about it this evening, Dick, as it is rather a long story."

After the Jacksons had driven off in the evening,

Dick again asked his father about the doings of Colonel Pearson's column.

"Well, my boy, they have neither suffered a great defeat, like that under Lord Chelmsford, nor obtained a decisive victory, like the column of Colonel Wood ; they have beaten the enemy in a fight, and are at present besieged in a place called Ekowe, or, as it is sometimes spelt, Etckowi. The column consisted of eight companies of the 3rd Buffs under Colonel Parnell; six companies of the 99th, under Colonel Welman ; one company of Royal Engineers and two 7-pounder guns; they had, besides a naval brigade consisting of 270 blue-jackets and marines of her Majesty's ships *Active* and *Tenedos*, with three gatling-guns, 200 mounted infantry ; 200 colonial mounted riflemen also formed part of the column, with about 2000 men of the native contingent. They had great difficulty in crossing the Tugela, which was nearly 400 yards wide. But, thanks to the exertions of the sailors, a flying bridge was constructed—that is, a boat with ropes attached to both shores, so that it can be pulled backwards and forwards, or, as is sometimes done, taken backwards and forwards by the force of the stream itself.

"It was the 13th before the crossing was effected. The enemy were in considerable force near the river. A small earthwork, called Fort Tenedos, was thrown up on the Zulu bank of the river. On the 18th the leading division started on its march into the enemy's country, followed the next day by the second division, a small detachment being left to garrison the fort.

Every precaution was taken in the advance, and the cavalry scouted the country in front of the column. At the end of the first day's march the Inyoni, a small stream ten miles north of the Tugela, was reached.

"The second day they encamped on the Umsin-dusi. The third day's march brought the column to the Amatikulu; beyond this the country became covered with bush, and great care was then taken, as it was known that a large force was marching from Ulundi to oppose their farther advance. Early on the morning of the 22nd, the day which proved so fatal to Colonel Glyn's column, the first division had just crossed the Inyezane River and was halted for breakfast, when they were attacked by a large force of the enemy, who, having chosen this position, were lying in wait for them. The ground chosen for the halt was not a favourable one, as it was surrounded by bush. But as no other place could be found by Major Barrow, who commanded the horse, near water, the halt had been made here. Scarcely had they begun their preparations for breakfast, when Captain Hart, who was out scouting in front with the advance company of the native contingent, discovered the enemy advancing rapidly over the ridge in his front and attempting to gain the bush on both flanks of the halting-place. The Zulus at once opened a heavy fire upon the native contingent, and of these one officer and four non-commissioned officers and three men fell almost immediately.

"The native contingent was called in, and the naval brigade and two guns, under Lieutenant Lloyd, and two companies of the Buffs were ordered to take up a position upon a knoll close to the road, on which they were halted. The sailors at once opened fire on the enemy with two 7-pounders and two 24-pounder rocket-tubes, while the Buffs poured a heavy fire with their rifles upon them. The waggons were still coming up, and these were parked as they reached the ground; and two companies of the Buffs, who were guarding them on the march, being now free to act, were ordered to move out in skirmishing order, and draw the enemy out of the bush, when, as they retired, they were exposed to the fire from the knoll.

"The engineers and mounted troops moved forward, with the infantry skirmishers, supported by a half-company of the Buffs and a half-company of the 99th. The enemy tried to outflank their left, and Captain Campbell with a portion of the naval brigade and some of the native contingent went out and drove them from a kraal of which they had taken possession. A still farther advance was now made, and the Zulus took to flight, leaving 300 dead upon the ground. The attacking party were 5000 strong, and against these some 500 or 600 of our troops were engaged. We had only eight Europeans killed and four natives, and about twenty wounded. The next day Colonel Pearson reached Ekowe. The position was a strong one, as the place stood upon rising ground; it had been a missionary station, and there was a church which could at the worst be converted into a citadel.

"Colonel Pearson at once set to work to fortify the position. The same evening the news arrived of the disaster at Isandula. After a consultation with his officers Colonel Pearson decided to hold the spot at which he now was, convinced that, without further supplies of reinforcements, he could hold the place for two months. In order to economize food, the mounted men and most of the natives were sent back, and there remained 1200 British troops.

"Colonel Pearson at once commenced his preparations for a siege. Three moderate-sized brick erections were turned into store-houses, and the church into a hospital, the tower making a capital look-out; from this a splendid view was obtained, the hill by the Tugela being clearly visible. The men set to work to fortify the place. The intrenchments were of a six-sided form, about sixty yards across, with a ditch outside them eighteen feet deep and twelve feet wide. Assegais were planted in the bottom. Added to the south side was a kraal for cattle and horses, also defended by a small wall. Outside the fort were entanglements of rows of felled trees and bushes. The supply of water was obtained from a good well, outside the walls, but covered by the fire of the fort. The guns were placed in position, and the garrison was ready for any attack that might be made upon them. All these details we learned in the early days of the siege by occasional messengers, who managed to find their way through, but these had been few and far between; of twelve messengers sent out the first week of February, only one got through. The garrison had made several sorties, and had destroyed Dabulamanzi's kraal. They also went out and cut off a large convoy of cattle on its way to Ulundi."

"But how have they found out what is being done at Ekowe, if the first week only one messenger got through out of twelve?" Dick said.

"By a very ingenious plan, Dick. For three weeks we knew nothing of what was going on, and then it struck an engineer that communication might be established by flashing signals."

"What are flashing signals, father?"

"Well, my boy, as a general rule they are made by showing a light either for a long or short period. Thus, one long and one short might be A; one short and one long, B; two short and one long, C; and so on all through the Alphabet. The distance was so great that ordinary lights would not have answered, but it struck one of the engineers that with a looking-glass the sunlight might be reflected. You know at what a distance the sun's reflection on a window can be made out. Well, it was tried in vain for a whole week by Lieutenant Haynes, of the Royal Engineers, but at the end of that time he was delighted at seeing answering flashes from the hill on which Ekowe stands. Since that time news has been regularly received every day by this means of what is passing in the fort.

" In the meantime preparations were being made for the relief of the garrison. The news of the defeat at Isandula was sent home by a swift ship, by which the particulars were telegraphed from St. Vincent. The people at home did not lose an hour. The *Shah*, which was on her way home, heard the news at St. Helena, and Captain Bradshaw, who commanded her, at once, on his own responsibility, turned his ship's head south, and steered for Durban, bringing with him the garrison of the island. Some draughts from the 4th, 88th, and 99th Regiments were brought down from the Cape; the *Boadicea* also arrived, and every man who could be spared from her and the *Shah* was landed and sent up to the Tugela.

" In the second week in March the 57th and 91st Regiments arrived from England. One hundred and sixty men were brought over from the garrison of Mauritius, and a few days later the 3rd battalion of the 60th Regiment also arrived. These assembled on the Tugela on the 27th, and that day set out. The vanguard was composed of the seamen and marines of the *Shah* and *Tenedos*—640 men and two gatlings, the 91st regiment of 900 men, 400 men of the 99th, 180 men of the 3rd Buffs, 150 mounted infantry, 200 of the mounted native contingent, and 1600 men of the native infantry contingent. The second division consisted of 200 men of the *Boadicea* with gatlings, the 37th Regiment, and the 3rd battalion of the 60th, 900 men, and two troops of mounted natives. That is all I can tell you, my boy. The news only arrived here yesterday that they had started. In the course of three or four more days I hope that we shall hear that they have given the Zulus a thorough licking. It is a strong force, and as there are about 3300 white troops among them, and there is no fear of their being taken by surprise this time, we need not have any anxiety about the result. I understand that, in accordance with the advice which Colonel Pearson has flashed from Ekowe, they are not going to follow the road he took, but to keep along on the lower ground near the sea."

"And do you think, father, that they will push on for Ulundi when they have rescued the garrison of Ekowe?"

"No, Dick; I think they are quite strong enough to do so, but as there are at least half a dozen more regiments on their way out from England, including some regiments of cavalry, it will be more prudent to stop until our whole fighting force is here, when we ought to be enabled to make short work of them, and to do the work completely and effectually. And now, Dick, I am thoroughly sleepy—the sooner we are in bed the better."

CHAPTER VIII.

THE SECOND ADVANCE.

IT was some days before the news reached Newcastle of the complete success of the relieving column. On their first day's march no difficulty was met with. The road was a good one, and the Zulus did not show in any force. The column halted for the night near the junction of the Inyoni and Amatikulu rivers. The waggons were placed in laager and a ditch and parapet formed round the camp. The ground was open and the waggons were able to travel six abreast. Numerous Zulu kraals were passed, but these were found deserted.

On the afternoon of the 1st they encamped at Ginghilovo. From this point Ekowe was visible; signals were exchanged with the besieged, and Colonel Pearson warned Lord Chelmsford that the Zulus were moving forward to attack him. The night passed quietly, but the greatest vigilance was maintained.

At daybreak dense masses of Zulus were seen in the distance, and at six o'clock they approached the camp. They came on in their usual order, with a massive centre and advanced horns on either flank. The British were kept lying down behind the shallow trenches they had thrown up. The Zulus advanced in splendid order with a sort of dancing step. Their white and coloured shields, their crests of leopard skins and feathers, and the long ox-tails dangling from their necks gave them a wild and strange appearance. Every ten or fifteen yards the first line would halt, a shot would be fired, then a loud yell burst forth, and they again advanced with a humming sound, in time to which their dancing movement was kept up. The 60th, who lay opposite to the point against which they advanced, withheld their fire until the first line of skirmishers came to within 300 yards. Then a deadly sheet of flame flashed along the ridge of the shelter-trench, and a number of the Zulu warriors fell.

The main body now rushed forward, and although a tremendous fusilade was kept up on them, the Zulu advance pressed on, ever fed by those in the rear, which deployed in excellent order as they reinforced the first line. For twenty minutes the fire of the 60th never ceased. Again and again the Zulus pressed forward, but their leading ranks were swept away by the storm of bullets.

At half-past six the Zulu masses, without the smallest confusion, faced to their right, ran round in columns, and fell upon the face of the laager held by the 57th and 91st. Here they were as hotly received as they had been by the 60th. Notwithstanding the deadly fire, the Zulus pressed forward with noble courage. They had ceased to shout now, and seemed only anxious to reach the square. Four times they rushed forward; each time they fell back with terrible loss. The fire of the soldiers was assisted by that of the native contingent, who, posted in the waggons behind, added their fire to that of the 91st and 57th.

The last attack was led by Dabulamanzi in person, and arrived within five yards of the muzzles of the men's rifles; indeed one or two of the chiefs actually seized the hot barrels with one hand, while they stabbed at the men with their shortened assegais.

This was their final repulse, and they now began to fall back. The moment that they did so, the cavalry dashed out in pursuit, and chased them far across the plain. The gatlings and 9-pounders added in no slight degree to the effect of the rifles. The entire English loss was but two officers and four privates killed, and three officers and thirty-four privates wounded; while the Zulu loss exceeded 1000. The force under Dabulamanzi was about 11,000, and a similar force was close at hand, but fortunately had not joined that of Dabulamanzi before he attacked the British.

On the following day the 57th, 60th, and 91st, together with the mounted men and several of the mounted brigade, taking with them three days' provisions, marched for Ekowe. Major Barrow scouted the ground, and reported that everywhere assegais, shields, feathers, ear and head ornaments, skins, furs, blankets, and even guns were lying about in confusion,

evidently cast away in their headlong flight by the
Zulus, but that none of these had been seen.

The column, however, advanced with every precaution, as it was possible that Dabulamanzi might procure reinforcements. No enemy, however, was met
with, and the column continued its march until they
were met by Colonel Pearson with 500 men, coming
out to lend a hand to them in case they should be
attacked. The united column then marched into
Ekowe. The health of the garrison had suffered
much from exposure to the sun and rain, and from
the want of vegetables and useful medicine. Beef
they had plenty of, as it was considered advisable
to kill and consume the waggon-oxen rather than see
them die from want of forage.

The great event of the siege had been the discovery
of certain strange flashes of light on the white walls
of the church-tower ; these, after puzzling many of the
officers and soldiers, were at length brought under
the notice of an officer of the naval brigade, who had
been trained in the use of the heliograph, and he was
able at once to explain the mystery. They were
three days before they could contrive an apparatus,
which could be worked, to reply. Fortunately an old
mirror was found, and communication was opened.
The effect of their renewed intercourse with the outer
world, and of learning the preparations which were
being made for their relief, acted more beneficially on
the health of the imprisoned garrison than all the
tonics the hospital could afford. Nevertheless between

the commencement of the siege and the arrival of the relief thirty deaths had occurred.

To the great regret of the garrison they found that it had been determined by the general to abandon the fort which they had held so long, as the whole force was required in Natal for operations in the field in conjunction with the reinforcements on their way out. Before leaving, however, it was determined to strike another blow at Dabulamanzi, whose private residence had escaped at the time that his kraal was burnt. A small party of about 200 men therefore went out and fired the place without resistance. Ekowe was evacuated, and, having left a garrison at Ginghilovo, Lord Chelmsford retired with his force across the Tugela.

Every day for the next fortnight news reached Newcastle of the arrival of one or more transports with reinforcements, and in a month from the date of the arrival of the first from England, seventeen transports came in, bringing more than 9000 soldiers and 2000 horses. The force consisted of two regiments of cavalry, 1250 sabres, two batteries of artillery with 540 men, 190 men of the Royal Engineers, six regiments of infantry, 5320 bayonets, draughts of the regiments already in the colony and Army Service Corps' men, 1200. Most of the regiments brought their equipments complete and ready for the field—tents, waterproof-sheets, cooking utensils, and camp stores. The Army Service Corps brought with them 100 light but strongly-built waggons.

Among the arrivals was the Prince Imperial of France, who had come out as a volunteer.

To convey the baggage and stores of so numerous a force an immense number of waggons was required, and a very urgent appeal was made to the loyalty of the colonists to furnish transport for the troops engaged in fighting their battles.

In answer to this appeal Mr. Humphreys and Mr. Jackson decided to send down the new waggons which had just been finished. Immediately they heard of the decision, Dick and Tom begged for permission again to accompany the waggons. Their mothers at first refused even to listen to the request, but their fathers, talking the matter over between them, agreed that harm was not likely this time to come of it.

The force was so overwhelmingly strong that there was not the slightest prospect of a repetition of the disaster of Isandula. At that time several hundred English soldiers had been surprised and crushed by some 20,000 of the enemy, but in future every precaution would be taken, and the British force would be ten times as strong as that which fought at Isandula. The colonists thought that it would be really an advantage to the boys to take part in the expedition; it was quite possible that if they remained in the colony they might have occasion to take part in wars with one or other of the native tribes, and the experience that they would gain in the campaign would in that case assuredly be useful to them.

Having thus decided, Mr. Humphreys and his friend succeeded in obtaining their wives' consent to the boys accompanying the waggons, and in high glee they started for Durban on the 20th of April.

The campaign was arranged on a new plan. The numerous columns in which the strength of the force had been frittered away were abolished, and the following was adopted as the designation of the forces in the field, under the lieutenant-general commanding, viz.:—1st Division South African Field-forces, Major-General Crealock, C.B., commanding, consisting of all troops on the left bank of the Lower Tugela; 2nd Division South African Field-forces, Major-General Newdigate commanding, consisting of all troops in the Utrecht district other than those attached to the Flying Column under Brigadier-General Wood, V.C., C.B., which was designated as "Brigadier-General Wood's Flying Column." Major-General Marshall assumed command of the cavalry brigade, and Major-General the Hon. H. H. Clifford, C.B., V.C., took up the command of the base of operations and superintendence of the lines of communication.

The forces were divided as follows :—

FIRST DIVISION (GENERAL CREALOCK'S),
LOWER TUGELA COMMAND.

Naval Brigade	800
M. Battery, 6th Brigade, Royal Artillery	90
Detachment, 11-7th Royal Artillery .	25
2-3rd Regiment	836

57th Regiment	830
3-60th „	880
88th „	640
91st „	850
99th „	870
Mounted Infantry, 2nd Squadron .	70
Army Service Corps	50
Army Hospital Corps . . .	20
Royal Engineers	150
8-7th Royal Artillery . . .	80
O-6th „ „	50
Lonsdale's Horse	84
Cooke's Horse	78
Colonial Volunteers	105
Native Contingent :—	
Foot	2556
Mounted	151
Total strength, effective and non-effective	9215

SECOND DIVISION (GENERAL NEWDIGATE'S.)

1st Dragoon-Guards } attached to .	650
17th Lancers } 2nd Division .	626
N-5th Royal Artillery . . .	76
N-6th „	80
10-7th „	70
10-6th „	30
Royal Engineers	60
2-4th Regiment	790
Detachment, 1-13th Regiment . .	63
2-21st (two companies at Maritzburg)	820

1-24th Regiment	530
2-24th „	586
58th (one company at Durban) . .	906
80th (several companies in the Transvaal)	300
94th (one company at Grey Town) .	870
Army Service Corps	60
Army Hospital Corps . . .	30
Grey Town District Colonial Volunteers	139
Natal Mounted Police . . .	75
Natal Carabineers	27
Newcastle Mounted Rifles .	18
Buffalo Mounted Guard . . .	20
Native Contingent :—	
Europeans	41
Natives (foot)	3128
Natives (mounted)	243
Total strength, effective and non-effective	10,238

GENERAL WOOD'S FLYING COLUMN.

11-7th Royal Artillery . . .	87
Royal Engineers	13
1-13th Regiment	721
90th „	823
1st Squadron, Mounted Infantry .	103
Army Service Corps	9
Army Hospital Corps . . .	13
Frontier Light Horse . . .	173

Baker's Horse	179
Transvaal Rangers	141
1st Battalion, Wood's Irregulars :—	
Europeans	14
Natives	377
2nd Battalion, Wood's Irregulars :—	
Europeans	5
Natives	355
Natal Native Horse :—	
Europeans	4
Natives	75
Total strength, effective and non-effective	3092

GRAND TOTAL.

1st Division	9215
2nd ,, ...	10,238
General Wood's Flying Column .	3092
Total, effective and non-effective : namely, Europeans, 15,660, and natives, 6885	22,545

Out of this grand total there were about 400 sick and non-effective with the 1st Division, 300 with the 2nd Division, and 600 (including some of Wood's Irregulars, absent and not accounted for since the 28th of March) with Wood's Flying Column. So that altogether, deducting, say, 1500, Lord Chelmsford had at his disposal, from the middle of April, a total of 21,000 troops, of which over 15,000 were European. Colonels Pearson and Wood were made brigadier-generals, and the former was to command No. 1

Brigade, 1st Division, and Colonel Pemberton, 3-60th, the other. They both, however, had to give up their commands through sickness, and Colonels Rowland, V.C., C.B., and Clark, 57th Regiment, succeeded them

Major-General Clifford, V.C., C.B., had the following staff for the management of the base of the operations and the maintenance of the lines of communication between Zululand and Natal :—

Lieutenant Westmacott, 77th Foot, aide-de-camp; Major W. J. Butler, C.B., assistant-adjutant and quartermaster-general, stationed at Durban; and Captain W. R. Fox, Royal Artillery, deputy assistant-adjutant and quartermaster-general.

On the arrival of the boys with the waggons at Pieter-Maritzburg, they reported themselves at the headquarters of the transport corps, and were told that they were not to go down to Durban, but were to load up at once and accompany the Dragoon-Guards, who were to march the next morning for the front.

This time the lads were mounted, as their fathers thought that they would gain more benefit from their experience if they were able to move about instead of being confined to the sides of their waggons, and it was a satisfaction to their mothers that, in case of any untoward event again happening, they would be in a better position for making their escape.

General Newdigate's columns were encamped at Landmann's Drift; the cavalry, under General Marshall, was also there. The march was altogether without incident.

Some days passed quietly, when a small party of

horse made an expedition to Isandula ; they reported that nearly a hundred waggons were still standing upon the field of battle. On the 17th of May, three days later, the rumour ran through the camp that the cavalry were to start on the 19th, to bury the dead and bring away the waggons. The Army Service Corps and waggons were to accompany the party, which was to consist of the Dragoon-Guards and Lancers, with a party of native mounted scouts.

In the afternoon of the 18th the two boys went to Colonel Marshall's tent ; they waited patiently until he came out, accompanied by two or three other officers.

" We have come to ask, sir, if you will allow us to go with your column. We are in charge of waggons here, but they are not going. We were at the battle, and saw the whole thing, and were taken prisoners afterwards and carried to Umbelleni's kraal, where we were liberated when Colonel Wood's cavalry attacked the Zlobani hill. We are well mounted, sir, and are good shots ; so, if you will let us go, we could keep with the scouts and not be in your way."

" How did you see the fight ? " General Marshall asked.

" We had gone up to the top of the hill, sir, before it began, and fortunately the natives did not notice us."

" Oh, yes, you can go," the general said. " Probably you can give us a better account of the action than and one else, as others who escaped were occupied by their own business, and could not mark the general progress of the battle. So you were taken prisoners! Well, I am going out now, but if you will call in this evening at about half-past eight, I shall be glad to have a talk with you."

In the evening the boys called upon the general, one of the most popular and dashing officers in the service. Three or four of his staff were there, and all listened with great interest to the boys' account of their adventures.

"You seem to have plenty of pluck and coolness, youngsters," the general said, when they had finished. "In future you need not trouble to ask for permission to accompany me whenever the cavalry go out, providing we have natives mounted with us; you must go as recruits, and can either keep with them or ride with my orderlies."

Much pleased with the permission given, the lads returned to the waggons, and the next morning they started on their way.

The column bivouacked that night at Dill's Town, and reached Rorke's Drift between three and four o'clock in the morning, and were there joined by the Natal Carabineers and Colonel Harness, R.A., with guns.

At daybreak on the 20th the reconnoitring force crossed the river. No signs of the enemy were seen until they neared Isandula; then signal-fires blazed up on the hills to the right, and spread quickly from hill to hill far into the interior. Pushing steadily on, the plain of Isandula was reached by ten

o'clock. The whole scene of the conflict was overgrown
with long grass, thickly intermixed with growing crops
of oats and Indian corn. Lying thickly here, and scattered over a wide area, lay the corpses of the soldiers,
The site of the camp itself was marked by the
remains of the tents, intermingled with a mass ol
broken trunks, boxes, meat-tins, papers, books, and
letters in wild disorder. The sole visible objects,
however, rising above the grass, were the waggons, all
more or less broken up.

The scouts were placed in all directions to give
warning of the approach of any enemies. The
Army Service Corps set to work to harness the
seventy pairs of led horses they had brought
with them to the best of the waggons, and the
troops wandered over the scene of the engagement,
and searched for and buried all the bodies they
found, with the exception of those of the 24th Regiment, as these, Colonel Glyn had asked, should be left
to be buried by their comrades. The bodies of the
officers of Colonel Durnford's corps were all found
together, showing that when all hope of escape was
gone they had formed in a group and defended themselves to the last. The men of the Royal Artillery
buried all the bodies of their slain comrades who
could be found, but the shortness of the time and the
extent of the ground over which the fight had extended
rendered anything like a thorough search impossible.

The object of the expedition was not to fight, and
as at any moment the Zulus might appear in force

upon the field, a start was made as soon as the waggons were ready. Forty of the best waggons were brought out, with some water-carts, a gun-limber and a rocket-battery cart. Twenty waggons in a disabled condition were left behind. Some seventy waggons were missing, these having been carried off by the Zulus, filled either with stores or with their own wounded. Having accomplished this work the cavalry rejoined headquarters at Land-mann's Drift.

On the 27th of May the column advanced, New-digate's division leading the way. By two o'clock in the afternoon the men had crossed the Buffalo and marched to Kopje-allein through a bare and tree-less country. One of the most popular figures in the camp was the Prince Imperial of France, who, having received a military education at Woolwich, and being anxious to see service, had applied for and obtained leave to accompany the expedition. The young prince had been extremely popular at Woolwich, and was indeed an immense favourite with all who knew him —high-spirited and full of life, and yet singularly gentle and courteous in manner. He was by nature adapted to win the hearts of all who came in contact with him. His abilities too were of the very highest order, as was proved by the fact that, although suf-fering under the disadvantage of being a foreigner, he yet came out so high in the final examination at Woolwich as to be entitled to a commission in the Royal Engineers. When it is considered how keen is the competition to enter Woolwich, and that all the students there, having won their places by competitive examinations, may be said to be considerably above the average of ability, it will be seen that, for one who had previously gone through an entirely different course of education, and had now to study in a language that was not his own, to take rank among the foremost of these was a proof both of exceptional ability and industry.

A splendid career was open for the young prince, for there is little doubt that, had he lived, he would sooner or later have mounted the throne of his father, and there are few pages of history more sad than those which relate to his death in a paltry skirmish in a corner of Africa. To Englishmen the page is all the more sad, inasmuch as, had the men accompanying him acted with the coolness and calmness generally shown by Englishmen in a moment of danger, instead of being carried away by a cowardly panic, the Prince Imperial might yet be alive.

At Kopje-allein Newdigate's column was joined by that of General Wood. Three days were spent in carefully exploring the country, and on the 1st of June the division, as nearly as possible 20,000 strong, with a baggage-train of 400 native waggons, moved forward and encamped near the Itelezi River. The flying column of General Wood went on one march ahead, and the country was carefully scouted by Buller's horse for twenty miles round, and no Zulus were found.

CHAPTER IX.

ULUNDI.

ON Sunday, the 1st of June, General Wood with a small escort was out reconnoitring in advance of his column, which was about five miles in front of the force of General Newdigate. The morning was clear and fresh, the ridges of the hills on either side were dotted with Buller's horsemen. They crossed the river by a ford, and having ridden about another mile forward they observed some of the vedettes on the high ground signalling that horsemen were approaching.

Riding on to see who they could be, they were joined by Colonel Buller and a dozen of his men, and together they rode forward to meet the five men who were seen approaching. In a few seconds Lieutenant Carey and four troopers of Bettington's Horse rode up, and when they had told their story English soldiers had the shame and humiliation of knowing that an English officer and four English troopers had escaped unwounded from a Zulu ambush, in which they had left a gallant young prince, the guest of England and the hope of France, to be barbarously slain.

Early in the morning the prince had learnt that a

patrol was to be sent out in advance of the column, and had applied for and obtained permission to accompany it. Colonel Harrison, acting as quartermaster-general, granted the permission, and had an interview with the prince.

Six men of Bettington's Horse and the same number of Shepstone's Basutos were to form the party; but unfortunately the Basutos did not come up at the appointed time, and the patrol consisted therefore only of the prince, Lieutenant Carey, the six men of Bettington's Horse, and one Zulu. Considering the importance of the safety of the prince, a grave responsibility attaches to the staff-officer who allowed him to go with so small a party.

After an hour's ride they reached the crest of a hill and dismounted to fix the position of some distant points by the compass. Here Colonel Harrison overtook them, and remarked that the whole of the escort was not with them, and that they had better wait for the Basutos to come up. The prince said,—

" Oh, we are quite strong enough—besides, we have all our friends around us, and with my glass I can see General Marshall's cavalry coming up."

Unfortunately Colonel Harrison did not insist that the party should wait until the Basutos arrived, and they proceeded another seven miles, and then halted in an isolated kraal in a valley. A worse spot could not have been selected for a halt, as it was surrounded by long grass, six or seven feet high; here the saddles were taken off the horses, and coffee was prepared.

Without any search being made they sat down to make coffee, although it was clear, from the burnt embers, bones, and other *débris*, that the place had been but recently occupied.

The Zulu was the first to see the enemy in the long grass, and the horses were at once saddled. The escort stood ready by them, and just as the prince gave the word, " Prepare to mount," the Zulus' war-cry burst out, and some guns were fired from the grass.

The horses started at the outburst, and some broke away. Never were a body of troops in an enemy's country so unprepared for the attack. Not a carbine was loaded! not a sentry placed! Each of the troopers, including the officer, was seized with a wild panic, and thought only of flight,—one indeed had fallen at the first shot. The prince's horse was ill-tempered and badly broken, and, frightened by the firing and yells, he was so restive that the prince was unable to mount. Had one of those men stood for an instant at his head the prince might have gained his saddle, but all had galloped away, leaving him alone. Running by his horse, he in vain endeavoured to mount; he had not had time to tighten the girth, the saddle slipped round, and the horse galloped away. Unfortunately the prince's revolvers were in the holsters, so he was unarmed, save with his sword, and with this he stood bravely at bay, and died nobly facing his foes, who pierced him with assegais at a distance.

According to Zulu accounts afterwards obtained,

there were but five or six men engaged in the attack, and had the Englishmen accompanying the prince, nay even had one of them, possessed but the smallest amount of presence of mind and courage, the Prince Imperial might have been saved. There is no blacker page in the annals of English military history.

The feeling of indignation, shame, and regret in the English camp, when this shameful episode was known, was indescribable. Of all the party the friendly Zulu was the only one who came out with honour; he had gone towards the river to fetch water when he discovered the enemy, and might have instantly taken flight. He returned, however, and gave warning that the Zulus were lurking round. Even then it does not appear that he attempted to fly, but fought the foe until overcome by numbers. His body was afterwards discovered not far from that of the prince, riddled with wounds, together with a number of his own assegais broken, but stained with the blood of his assailants.

The next morning the cavalry rode out to find and bring in the prince's body. When it was discovered, it was tenderly brought into camp. It was afterwards taken over to England, and laid by the remains of his father at Chislehurst. A court-martial was held on Lieutenant Carey. The sentence was kept secret, but it was generally understood that he was dismissed from the service with ignominy. He was sent home under arrest, but on his arrival there the proceedings of the court-martial were declared null and void on account of some technical irregularity, and he was ordered to resume his duties. It was reported that this extraordinary leniency was shown by the special desire of the Empress, who made a personal request to the Queen that nothing should be done in the matter.

Early in June some messengers arrived in Lord Chelmsford's camp from Cetewayo. Lord Chelmsford told them that before any negotiations could be entered into, the whole of the spoil taken at Isandula, especially the two captured 7-pounder guns, must be restored.

Considerable delays now took place, and for three weeks a force of Englishmen sufficient to march through and through Zululand in every direction was kept doing nothing at a distance of three days' march from the enemy's capital. So extraordinary and unaccountable was the delay that the English government appointed Sir Garnet Wolseley to go out to supersede Lord Chelmsford. Upon the receipt of this news preparations for an advance were at last made. On the 21st General Newdigate's column reached the right bank of the Umlatoosi. General Crealock, who commanded the division which was operating by the sea, also moved forward about this time, but met with such difficulties, owing to the sickness which attacked his transport-train, that he was unable to co-operate with the first division, although his force did service by occupying a large number of the enemy, who would otherwise have been free to act against the main column

Between the 24th and 26th General Newdigate's and Wood's columns advanced but six miles. But Buller with his horse scouted ahead, and cut up a number of Zulus who were engaged in burning the grass, to hinder the advance of the horses and cattle. On the 26th Colonel Drury-Lowe, with the light cavalry, 450 of Buller's men and two guns, went out and attacked and burnt five large military kraals. On the 27th the column advanced five miles towards Ulundi, leaving their tents behind them, and taking only 200 ammunition-waggons and ten days' rations; 500 infantry were left to guard the stores.

On the afternoon of that day some messengers came in from Cetewayo, bringing 150 of the cattle captured at Isandula, together with a pair of elephant's tusks, and a letter written in English by a trader captured at Isandula. The letter said that the king could not comply with all Lord Chelmsford's commands, as the arms taken from us at Isandula were not brought to him, and that it was beyond his power as a king to order or compel any of his regiments to lay down their arms. He said the cannons should be sent in, and on the receipt of the cattle and these weapons the English must retire from Zululand. The trader had written in a corner of the letter, in pencil, a few words of warning, and an intimation that Cetewayo had with him at Ulundi a picked force of 20,000 men.

Lord Chelmsford refused to receive the tusks, and told the messengers to inform Cetewayo, that before he should think of retiring, all the conditions must be complied with, and the Zulu regiments lay down their arms. Late in the evening several large bodies of the enemy, amounting to some thousands, were noticed moving from the direction of Ulundi, passing by their left flank.

The next morning General Wood moved forward as far as the left bank of the White Umvolosi, and Newdigate's column followed in the afternoon. Wood's division bivouacked on the farther side of the river, Newdigate's halted on the right. The most vigilant watch was kept, with pickets in every direction, and patrols of cavalry beyond these.

At daybreak on the 27th the main body crossed the river, and joined Wood on the left bank. They were now but fifteen miles from Ulundi, and the king's five kraals were visible to the naked eye. Three days were given to Cetewayo to comply with the conditions, but the original terms were altered so far, that Lord Chelmsford consented to receive 1000 captured rifles instead of insisting upon the regiments laying down their arms. While waiting, the army remained on the Umvolosi, having retired to the right side, pending the decision of peace or war.

During these three days the Zulus had made many hostile demonstrations against us. On the first and second they kept up a scattered fire at distant ranges at our men, and on the third, growing bolder, pushed their skirmishers down to the rocks on the opposite side of the river, and fired upon the men, as they were watering their horses in the stream. One horse was killed and several men wounded.

Buller therefore asked and obtained permission to make a raid on the other side. A couple of guns were brought into requisition to defend his crossing, and two or three rounds of shrapnel sent a crowd of Zulus, who had approached the opposite heights, straggling in all directions. Buller's horse, the mounted infantry, and Baker's horse dashed over the river at once. At full speed they raced across the country; Baker's men, guided by their leader, inclined to the left front, by Buller's orders, to carry and hold a hillock which commanded the ford.

Colonel Raaf, with a portion of Buller's horse, was halted near the kraal of Unodwingo to act as a reserve, and Buller, with 100 of his best mounted men, pushed on with the intention of exploring the ground as far as possible towards Ulundi. He knew that the bulk of the king's army was away upon Lord Chelmsford's right flank, and thought therefore that he might push on to Ulundi without opposition. The country consisted of a plain, across which ran some stony undulations, and at one point were two hollows, united at a right angle. The Zulu general disposed his men in shelter, and as Buller with his little band of horsemen rode up they rose and poured a very heavy fire into the ranks of the horsemen. Sudden and unexpected as was this attack, Buller's men were too well used to native fighting to evince the slightest confusion. In the most perfect order they began to fall back in alternate ranks, keeping up a steady fire upon the enemy, who were eagerly advancing. Raaf and his men rode up to the assistance of the hotly-pressed party, and Baker's horse, upon their hillock, opened a steady fire upon the Zulus. Gradually and steadily the cavalry fell back towards the river, the two guns on the opposite bank aiding them by their fire of grape and shrapnel upon the Zulus, who pressed forward with extreme bravery.

Many gallant deeds were done. Lord William Beresford, who had accompanied the party as a volunteer, distinguished himself by his bravery and coolness. Seeing upon the ground a dismounted and wounded trooper, surrounded by a dozen Zulus, he wheeled his horse and dashed down among them, knocking over three with the rush of his horse, and cutting down two with right and left strokes of his sabre; in another moment he had the wounded man on his horse behind him, and carried him off in safety.

Commander D'Arcy, also seeing a wounded man on the ground, tried to carry him off, but his horse, being restive, reared and fell back upon him, so that the unfortunate trooper was overtaken and assegaied; while D'Arcy, who was severely bruised by falling on his revolver, was able to get back safely, but was unable to take part in the next day's fight.

A little before daybreak Wood with his flying column crossed the river, followed by the main army. The whole of the baggage was left in charge of the 24th, and nothing was taken, save the ammunition and water-carts, each man carrying four days' supply of biscuits and preserved meat in

his havresack. The crossing of the river was made
without any opposition, but the movements of the
troops were watched by a party of Zulus from a
hillock on the left.

As soon as favourable ground had been reached,
Wood was signalled to halt and wait for the main body,
and when the junction was effected the order was given
to form a large hollow square. Inside this square were
two companies of engineers, together with the ammu-
nition-carts, water-carts, and ambulance waggons,
carts with intrenching tools, stretchers and bearers,
together with two gatling-guns in a reserve. The
front face of the square was formed by the 80th
Regiment, with two gatling-guns in their centre and
two 7-pounders on their right. The right face of
the square was formed of seven companies of the 13th
Regiment. Next to these came two 7-pounder and
one 9-pounder guns; four companies of the 58th
completed the line on this side. The rear face was
composed of two companies of the 21st, and three
companies of the 94th, with a 9-pounder gun. On
the left or west flank were three companies of the 94th,
two 7-pounder guns, eight companies of the 90th,
and two 9-pounders. Buller's cavalry were away,
scouring the country on the flanks. Colonel Drury-
Lowe, with two squadrons of the 17th Lancers and
Captain Shepstone's Basutos, formed the rear-guard.
The square moved forward for a few miles, when they
began to near the smaller kraals. Towards the left
front the Zulu columns could now be seen across the
plain, with the sun glancing down upon their long lines

of white shields. Upon reaching the first kraal the square was halted while it was fired. The next kraal was a very large one, called Unodwingo. This was also fired; but, as it was found that the smoke drifted across the plain so as to act as a screen to the Zulus, Lord Chelmsford ordered its extinction. Strong columns of the enemy could now be seen moving out in good order from Ulundi, and the square halted on some slightly-rising ground.

The Zulus soon opened a dropping fire on the right front, and from a strong force operating on some broken ground near Unodwingo on the left. By nine o'clock the Zulu attack was fairly developed. Buller's men then made a strong demonstration on the left, driving the Zulus from the hollow where they were sheltered back to the Unodwingo kraal. This movement was well supported by Shepstone and the Basutos.

The Zulus now brought up a strong reinforcement from the right, so as to assist those engaged with the cavalry. Buller's men fought in the Dutch fashion, in two ranks; the first mounted and ready to dash in a moment upon any weak point in the enemy's line, the second on foot, using their saddles as a rest for their rifles. As soon as the front rank became too hardly pressed, they cantered to the rear and dismounted and opened fire, while the second rank mounted in readiness to charge. Gradually Buller and Shepstone fell back, the Zulu column pressing upon them until well within reach of the gatlings and Martinis. The cavalry then took refuge in the square, and over the ridges

of the front and left the Zulu column with loud shouts
swept down upon the square. The British infantry now
opened fire. Gatlings and rifles poured in their deadly
hail of fire, while the guns swept the Zulu ranks with
shrapnel and grape. Terrible as the fire was, the
Zulus pressed bravely forward, filling up the gaps made
in their ranks, their wild war-cry rising even above
the roll of the rifle-fire. The fiercest attack came
from the Unodwingo kraal. Forming under cover of
the kraal, a large body, led by a chief on a white
horse, and formed in a hollow square, dashed at the
right rear angle of the British formation. Tremendous as the fire was, they pressed forward until it
seemed as if they would come to close quarters with the
column ; but, brave as the Zulus were, it was impossible
to withstand the fire which the 21st, 94th, 58th,
and Royal Engineers poured into them. The square
was broken up, and after a moment's pause the Zulus
turned and sought shelter from the leaden hail.

While the fight was raging here, another Zulu
column had attacked the front ; but here the assault
was speedily repulsed, the cool and steady fire of the
80th having so deadly an effect that the Zulus never
attempted to make a rush upon them. It was now
a quarter to ten—but a quarter of an hour from the
firing of the first shot, but the combat was virtually
at an end. The Zulus, astounded at the storm of fire
by which they had been received, were everywhere
wavering ; Lord Chelmsford gave the order, and the
two squadrons of lancers burst from the square,

greeted with a loud cheer from the infantry, and with their pennons fluttering in the breeze, and their long lances in rest they dashed upon the flying Zulus, and drove them headlong into a little ravine. But flanking this, and hidden by the long grass, half a Zulu regiment had been posted to cover the retreat, and as the squadrons of lancers came on a volley was poured in, which emptied several saddles and killed Lieutenant Wyatt-Edgell, who was leading his men. In another moment the line of lancers dashed down upon the Zulu ranks, and before the level line of lances the enemy went down like grass. Shattered and broken in an instant, the Zulus fought in stubborn knots, stabbing at the horses, throwing themselves on the men, and trying to dismount them.

In a *mêlée* like this the lance was useless, and the troopers drew their swords and fought hand to hand with the foe; and now a troop of the King's Dragoon-Guards and Buller's horse took up the charge, and the flying Zulus were cut down in scores before they could gain the crest of the hill. The Zulus here fought with far less determination than they had ex-hibited at Kambula. There for four hours they had striven in vain to carry General Wood's strongly-intrenched position; here they made one great effort, and then all was over. Their force was estimated at 23,000, and of these they lost only about 1500, of whom at least one-third were killed in the retreat. The battle over, the remaining kraals were burnt.

Most unfortunately, the day after the battle of

Ulundi, the news of the arrival of Sir Garnet Wolseley reached the front, and the movements of the army were paralyzed by the change of command. Instead therefore of a vigorous pursuit of the enemy, nothing was done, and the army halted until the new commander-in-chief should arrange his plans of action. Lord Chelmsford at once resigned command of his column, and left for England.

The two boys had been present at the battle of Ulundi. They had, during the weary weeks which preceded the advance, made the acquaintance of most of the officers of the cavalry, and Colonel Lowe had repeated the permission given them by General Marshall. They had therefore, when on the morning of the fight the column marched out, attached themselves to Shepstone's mounted Basutos, and had fought in the ranks of that corps during the cavalry action which preceded the attack on the square.

After the action was over, great quantities of cattle and corn fell into the hands of the troops, and so large a transport-train was no longer necessary. Orders were therefore issued that a certain number of the waggons could take their discharge from the service, and the lads at once applied to be placed on the list of those whose services could be dispensed with.

Two days later they started for the rear with a convoy of sick and wounded, and in due time, without further adventure, arrived home, to the great delight of their parents.

The victory of Ulundi virtually put an end to the

war ; a great portion of the troops were sent home ; the Zulu chiefs came in and surrendered with their followers, almost to a man. Cetewayo succeeded in concealing himself for some time, but after a long chase he was captured by Major Marter and Lord Gifford, and was sent a prisoner to the Cape.

CHAPTER X.

A TRADING EXPEDITION.

AFTER dividing Zululand into districts and appoint-
ing a chief to rule over each, General Wolseley
marched his force against Secoceni, the chief whose
hostile attitude had caused the Boers to accept the
protectorate of England. This chief had maintained his
defiant attitude, and, relying upon the strength of his
hill-stronghold, had kept up an irregular war upon
them, aided by the Swazis who came down from the
north to assist him.

Sir Garnet Wolseley attacked Secoceni's mountain.
His men fought bravely, but were altogether unable
to resist the attack of the English. The place was
carried, his warriors killed or dispersed, and his power
altogether broken. As the lads were not present at
this affair—being well contented to stay for a while
and assist their fathers in the farm—it is not necessary to enter into further details of it.

A few months later three teams of waggons drove
up to the farm. It was late in the evening, and their
owner, who had met Mr. Humphreys several times at
Newcastle, knocked at the door.

" I have made a long march," he said, "to-day, and
the oxen are knocked up; so if you will take me in,
I will halt here for the night instead of going on. The

roads have proved heavier than I had expected, and I have done a very long day's journey."

Mr. Humphreys at once invited the speaker to enter. Mr. Harvey was a trader, one of those who are in the habit of taking long expeditions far into the interior, with his waggons laden with cotton. beads, tower-muskets, powder, lead, and toys prized by the natives, returning laden with ivory, ostrich feathers, and skins. He was now about to start upon such a journey, having stocked his waggons at Durban.

After supper was over, the trader told many stories of his adventures among the natives, and the profits which were gained by such journeys.

"Generally," he said, "I go with six waggons, but I was very unlucky last time; the tzetze-fly attacked my animals, most of which died, and the natives took advantage of my position to make an attack upon me. I beat them off, but was finally obliged to pack all my most valuable goods in one waggon, to make my way back with it, and abandon everything else to the natives. Now, Humphreys, why don't you join me? You have got a waggon, and you can buy stores at Newcastle, not of course as cheap as at the seaside, but still cheap enough to leave a large marginal profit on the trip."

"I cannot leave the farm," Mr. Humphreys said.

"Nor can his wife spare him, Mr. Harvey," Mrs. Humphreys put in.

"Well, why don't you send your son, here, with the

waggon ?" Mr. Harvey asked. " The man who gene-rally travels with me as partner broke his leg the other day, down at Durban, and I should be very glad of one or two white companions. Two or three white men together can do anything with the natives, but if there is only one, and he happens to knock up, it goes very hard with him."

" Well, I don't know," Mr. Humphreys said, as Dick looked eagerly towards him ; " it is a sort of thing that wants thinking over."

" Oh ! father," Dick exclaimed excitedly, "it would be a glorious trip, especially if Tom Jackson would go too. I heard Mr. Jackson only yesterday say that his draught-oxen are eating their heads off, and that he must put them on the road to do some freighting. You see, if Mr. Jackson did not care about going in for the trading himself—and I know, from what he said the other day, that his money is all employed on the farm —you might hire his waggon for the trip. In fact that and your own—"

" That sounds easy and satisfactory enough, Dick," Mr. Humphreys said, laughing ; " but one does not jump into these things in a moment. There, you go off to bed, and I will talk the matter further over with Mr. Harvey."

Dick went to bed in high glee. When his father once said that he would talk a thing over, Dick felt that the chances were very strong that he would give in to his wishes. Mr. Humphreys was less influ-enced by the idea of making a good trading speculation than by the consideration that a journey of this kind would not only give great pleasure to his son, but would be of real benefit to him. It was Mr. Humphreys' opinion that it is good for a lad to be placed in positions where he learns self-reliance, readiness, and promptness of action. For himself his farm-work occupied all his thoughts, and he needed no distraction ; but for a lad change is necessary. Had Dick had—as would have been the case at home—a number of school-fellows and companions of the same age, he would have joined in their games and amusements, and no other change would have been necessary, or indeed desirable ; but in the farm in Natal it was altogether different. The work of looking after a number of Kaffirs planting and watering trees was monotonous, and unbroken, as it generally was, by the sight of a strange face from the beginning to the end of the week, it was likely to become irksome to a boy.

Occasionally indeed Dick and Tom Jackson would meet and go out on a shooting expedition together ; but Tom could seldom be spared, as his father, being shorter-handed than Mr. Humphreys, found him of considerable use.

Soon after daylight Dick was aroused by his father.

"Jump up at once, Dick ; I want you to ride over with a letter to Mr. Jackson. We have pretty well settled that you shall go with Mr. Harvey, and I am writing to make an offer to Mr. Jackson for the use of his waggon for six months."

Dick gave a shout of delight, and in a very short

time had dressed himself, and, having saddled his horse, was dashing at full speed across the veldt. Early as the hour was when he arrived, Mr. Jackson was already out in his fields. Dick soon found him, and handed him the letter, and while he was reading it explained in low, excited words to Tom the mission on which he had come.

"Well, I don't know," Mr. Jackson said, when he had finished the letter; "your father makes me a very liberal offer, Dick, for my waggon and team for six months, on the condition that I allow Tom to accompany them, and he points out that in his opinion a journey of this kind will be likely to develop the boy's character and teach him many things that may some day be of use to him. It comes upon me suddenly, and it seems he wants the waggon and team to be at Newcastle this evening, ready for a start in the morning. He himself is going to ride over there to purchase goods to freight it directly he receives my reply. I must go in and consult with mother before I come to any decided conclusion."

So saying he strode off towards the house.

Dick, leading his pony, walked after, by the side of Tom, to whom he explained all he knew of the character of the proposed journey.

"Mr. Harvey says, Tom, that of course he goes to trade, but that at the same time he does a lot of shooting, both for the sake of the skins and for the meat for the men. He says that he often meets with lions, hippopotami, and sometimes elephants—sometimes they meet with hostile natives."

Altogether the expedition promised an immense variety of adventure. The boys remained chatting outside the house until Mr. Jackson came to the door and called them in.

"So you are not contented to stop at home, Dick," Mrs. Jackson said, "and you want to take Tom rambling away with you again? Of course I cannot say no, when my husband is inclined to let him go, but I shall be terribly anxious until he is back again."

"I wont let him get into any scrapes, Mrs. Jackson," Dick said confidently.

"I have no faith whatever," Mrs. Jackson said, smiling, "in your keeping him out of scrapes, but I do think it possible that you may get him out of them after he is once in them. Do be careful, my boys, for the sakes of your fathers and mothers! I know Mr. Harvey has been making these journeys for a good many years and has always got back safely, and I have great faith in his experience and knowledge,—but there, Dick, I must not keep you. Here is my husband with an answer to your father's letter, and as you will have lots to do, and your father will be waiting for this letter before he starts for Newcastle, you had better ride off at once. Good-bye, my boy, for I shan't see you again before you start. I trust that you will come back safe and well."

Two minutes later Dick was again galloping across the country, arriving home in time for breakfast.

Mrs Humphreys was in better spirits than Dick

had feared he should find her; but her health had improved immensely since her arrival in the colony, and she was more active and energetic than Dick ever remembered her to have been. She was able therefore to take a far more cheerful view of the proposed expedition than she could have done the year before, and her husband had had comparatively little difficulty in obtaining her consent to Dick's accompanying Mr. Harvey.

"Your father thinks that it will be for your good, my boy," she said, "and I have no doubt that you will enjoy yourself greatly,—but be sure to be careful, and don't let your high spirits get you into scrapes;—remember how valuable your life is to us!"

"While you are away, Dick," his father said, "you will remember that you are absolutely under Mr. Harvey's orders. As the head of the expedition he stands in the position of the master, and he must receive ready and explicit obedience from all. He is not a man unnecessarily to curb or check you, and you may be sure that he will not restrain you unless for the good of the expedition. You must beware how far you stray from the caravan; the country you are going to is very different from this. Here, go where you will, you are sure in a short time to come upon some farmhouse, where you may get directions as to your way. There, once lost, it is upon yourself alone you must depend to recover the track. The beasts of prey are formidable opponents, and a lion or an elephant wounded, but not killed, could rend you into pieces in a moment; therefore you must be prudent as well as brave, obedient as well as enterprising. You have already shown that you have plenty of presence of mind, as well as of courage, and in nine cases out of ten the former quality is even the more necessary in a country such as that you are now going to. Courage will not avail you when a wounded leopard is charging down upon you, and your rifle is already discharged, but presence of mind may point out some means of escape from the danger. And now, if you have finished breakfast, you had better ride over with me to Newcastle—I have a very large number of goods to buy. Mr. Harvey, who went on the first thing, will meet me there and show me the kind of goods most likely to take with the natives; it will be well that you should not only know the price of each article, but that you should see everything packed, so as to know the contents of each bale by its shape and markings—a matter which may save you much trouble when you begin to trade."

The shopping did not take up so long a time as Mr. Humphreys had anticipated; the large store-keepers all kept precisely the kind of goods required, as they were in the habit of selling to the Boers for barter with the natives.

In the afternoon the waggon was sent away, and an hour before daybreak next morning Dick, having bade farewell to his mother, started with Mr. Humphreys.

Tom and Mr. Jackson arrived there a few minutes later, and the work of loading the waggons at once commenced, and was concluded by nine o'clock ; then they joined the waggons of Mr. Harvey, which were already waiting outside the town.

Their fathers rode with them to the ford across the river, and then after a hearty farewell returned to their farms, while the caravan of five waggons crossed into the Transvaal.

Each waggon was drawn by sixteen oxen, with a native driver and leader to each. There were three Swazis who had accompanied Mr. Harvey on previous expeditions, all good hunters and men who could be relied upon in every emergency. The eldest of these natives was a very tall and muscular man, of some five and forty years of age ; the left side of his face, his shoulder, and side were deeply seamed with scars, the relics of a fight with a wounded lioness. He had a very long and difficult name, which had been Anglicized and shortened by Mr. Harvey into "Jack."

The second of the trio was a man so short as to be almost deformed, a very unusual circumstance among the natives. His head was set low between his shoulders, and his long sinewy arms reached almost to his ankles. Mr. Harvey told the lads he was immensely strong, and the expression of his face was quick and intelligent. He was about twenty-four years of age ; he had been found by Mr. Harvey's father, who had also been a trader, deserted and apparently dying, a baby of only a few months old. Among savage people infants who are in any way deformed are generally deserted and left to perish, and this was the fate evidently intended for the child when the mother became convinced he would not grow up tall and straight, like other men. Mr. Harvey had picked it up, fed and cared for it, and it grew up full of a passionate attachment for him, following him everywhere, and ready at any moment to give his life for him. He was called Tony, and spoke English as fluently as the native language.

The third of the hunters was a tall, slight figure, a man of about five and thirty, with muscles like whipcord, who could, if it were needed, go for 100 miles without a halt, and tire out the swiftest horse. In addition to these were ten natives, who assisted with the cattle, pitched the tent, cooked and skinned the game, and did other odd jobs.

The road was fairly good, and two days after leaving Newcastle they arrived at Standerton, a rising place, inhabited principally by English traders and shopkeepers. Here three roads branched: the one led to Utrecht on the east; another to Pretoria, the capital, to the north-west; while the third, a track much less used than the others, led due north. This was the one followed by the caravan.

As they proceeded, the Dutch farmhouses became more sparsely sprinkled over the country, and several large native kraals were passed. Over the wide plains large herds of deer roamed almost unmolested, and the lads had no difficulty in keeping the caravan well supplied with provisions. One or two of the Kaffirs generally accompanied them, to carry in the game; but Mr. Harvey and the three hunters, accustomed to more exciting sport, kept along with the caravan, the former well content that the lads should amuse themselves with furnishing food for the party.

At Newcastle Mr. Humphreys had purchased a couple of small pocket-compasses, one for each of the boys, and the possession of these gave them great confidence, as, with their guidance, they were always enabled to strike the trail of the caravan.

The road had now altogether ceased, and they were travelling across a bare, undulating country, dotted occasionally by herds and flocks of Dutch settlers, and by the herds of wandering deer, but unbroken by a tree of any size, and for the most part covered with tall grass. The deer met with were for the most part antelopes of one or other of three kinds, all of which abound on the higher plains. These are known as the "wilde-beest," the "bless-buck," and the "spring-buck."

The venison which these creatures afforded was occasionally varied by the flesh of the "stump-pig," which abounded in considerable numbers, and, as they ran at a great speed, afforded the boys many a good chase.

Generally the caravan halted for the night—while they were still in a country occupied here and there by

Boers—near one of the farmhouses. It was not that these habitations added to the pleasure of the halting-place, for the Boers were generally gruff and surly, and their dogs annoyed them by their constant barking and growling, but for the most part it was only at these farmhouses that water could be obtained. A small sum was generally charged by the Boers for the privilege of watering the oxen of each waggon.

It would seem a churlish action to charge for water, but this fluid is very scarce upon the veldt. There are long periods of drought, of which, in a dry season, thousands of cattle perish ; it is therefore only natural that each farmer should hoard his supply jealously, for he cannot tell how great his own need of it may shortly be. The water is for the most part stored in artificial ponds, made by damming up hollows through which the water runs in the wet season.

Sometimes, as the caravan made its slow way along, a young Boer would dash up upon his horse, and, reining in, ask a few questions as to their route, and then ride off again. Already the boys had admired the figures and riding of the Boers whom they had seen in action in Zululand, but they were much more struck by their appearance as they saw them now. There are no finer men in the world than the young Boers of the Transvaal ; in after-life they often become heavy, but as young men their figures are perfect. Very tall and powerfully built, they sit their horses as if man and animal were one, and are such splendid marksmen that, while riding at full speed, they can, with almost absolute certainty, bring down an antelope at a distance of 150 yards.

But the abodes of the Boers, and their manner of living, impressed the boys far less favourably. However extensive the possessions and numerous the herds of a Boer, he lives in the same primitive style as his poorest neighbour. The houses seldom contain more than two, or at most three, rooms. The dress of the farmer, wife, and family is no better than that of labourers; whole families sleep in one room; books are almost unknown in their houses, and they are ignorant and prejudiced to an extreme degree. Upon his horse and his gun the Boer will spend money freely, but for all other purposes he is thrifty and close-fisted in the extreme. Water is regarded as useful for drinking purposes, but its utility for matters of personal cleanliness is generally altogether ignored. Almost all sleep in their clothes, and a shake and a stretch suffice for the morning toilet.

The power of a Boer over his sons and daughters is most unlimited, and he is the hardest and cruellest of masters to the unfortunate natives whom he keeps in slavery under the title of indentured apprentices, and whose lives he regards as of no more importance than those of his sheep, and as of infinitely less consequence than those of his horses or even of his dogs. To the unhappy natives the taking over of the Transvaal by England had been a blessing of the highest kind.

For the first time the shooting of them in cold blood had come to be considered a crime, and ordinances had been issued against slavery, which, although generally evaded by the Boers, still promised a happy state of things in the future.

At the native kraals the travellers were always welcomed when it was known that they were English. The natives looked to Queen Victoria as a sort of guardian angel, and not a thought entered their heads that they would ere long be cruelly and basely abandoned to the mercies of the Dutch by the government of England.

Slowly and without incident the caravan made its way north, and at last encamped upon the banks of the great river Limpopo, the northern boundary of the Transvaal. This river was too wide and deep to be forded, but at the spot where they had struck it, there was a large native kraal. Here Mr. Harvey, who had many times before followed the same route to this spot, was warmly welcomed, and preparations were made for effecting a crossing. The oxen were first taken across; these were steered by ropes attached to their horns and fastened to a canoe, which paddled ahead of them. The beasts were delighted to enter the water after their long dusty journey, and most of them, after reaching the opposite bank, lay down for a long time in the shallow water at the edge. Most of the stores were carried across in canoes. Inflated skins were then fastened to the waggons, and these also were towed across the stream by canoes. The passage had commenced at early morning, and by nightfall the whole of the caravan and its contents were safely across the stream.

"We are now," Mr. Harvey said, "in the Matabele country; the natives are for the most part friendly, as they know the advantage they derive from the coming of English traders, but there are portions of the tribe altogether hostile to us, and the greatest caution and care have to be exercised in passing through some portions of the country. To the east lies a land said to be very rich in gold, and there can be little doubt that it is so, for we frequently find natives who have traded with that country in possession of gold-dust, but they allow no white men to pass their frontier on any pretext whatever. They have become aware in some way how great is the value of gold in the eyes of Europeans, and fear that if the wealth of the country in that metal were but known a vast emigration of Europeans would take place, which would assuredly sooner or later end in the driving out or extirpation of the present inhabitants of the land."

The news which they had learned at the village where they had crossed, of the state of affairs among the tribes of the north, was not encouraging. The natives said that there had been much fighting. Not only had eruptions taken place with tribes still further north, but the Matabele had also been quarrelling among themselves.

"This is bad news indeed," Mr. Harvey said; "these

tribal wars make journeying very difficult; for, although none of the tribes may be hostile to Europeans at ordinary times, they view them with distrust when coming from a tribe with whom they are at war. In peace-time, too, when each section of the tribe is under some sort of control by the head chief, each will hesitate to rob or attack an European caravan, because the whole would consider themselves aggrieved and injured by such a proceeding. In war-time, on the other hand, each thinks, ' If we do not rob this rich caravan some one else is sure to do so; we may as well have the plunder as another.' War is injurious to us in other ways; instead of the tribes spending their time in hunting, they remain at home to guard their villages and women, and we shall find but little ivory and few ostrich feathers gathered to trade for our goods. I had not intended to have encumbered myself with a larger following, but I think, after what I have heard, it will be wise to strengthen our party before going further. I will therefore hire twenty men from the village here to accompany us; they will be useful in hunting, and will cost but little; their wages are nominal, and we shall have no difficulty in providing them with food with our rifles. In one respect they are more useful than men hired from time to time from among the people farther north for the purpose of driving game, for, as you see, many of them carry guns, while beyond the river they are armed only with bows and arrows."

" I am surprised to see so many guns," Dick said;

"where could these people have got the money to buy them?"

"It is the result of a very bad system," Mr. Harvey replied. "The Cape authorities, in spite of all the representations which have been made to them, of the extreme danger of allowing the natives to possess firearms, allow their importation and sale to them, simply on account of the revenue which they derive from it, as a duty of a pound is charged on each gun imported into the colony. From all parts of South Africa the natives, Pondos, Basutos, Zulus, and other Kaffirs, go to the diamond-fields and work there for months; when their earnings suffice to enable them to buy a gun, a stock of ammunition, and a blanket, they return to their homes. All these fellows you see carrying guns have served their six or eight months in the diamond-mines; a dozen of them would be a strong reinforcement to our fighting power, in case of an attack."

There was no difficulty in engaging the required number of men. Each was to be paid on the conclusion of the journey with a certain quantity of powder and lead, a few yards of cotton, some beads and other cheap trinkets, and was to be fed on the journey. Thus reinforced the caravan proceeded on its way.

CHAPTER XI.

A TROOP OF LIONS.

THE country across which the waggons now made their way differed somewhat from that over which they had previously passed ; it was not so undulating, and the herbage was shorter and more scanty ; the soil was for the most part sandy ; trees were much more abundant, and sometimes there were thick growths of jungle. Even before leaving the Transvaal they had at night often heard the roar of lions, but these had not approached the camp.

"We must look out for lions to-night," Mr. Harvey said, when the caravan encamped near a large pool which in the wet season formed part of a river, and was now for the most part dry. "We must laager our waggons, and get as many cattle inside as we can, and must keep the rest close together, with fires in readiness to light in case of an attack."

"But surely the lions would never venture to attack so large a party ?" Dick said in surprise.

"They will indeed," Mr. Harvey answered. "These brutes often hunt together, as many as twenty or thirty ; they are nothing like such powerful beasts as the North African lions, but they are formidable enough, and the less we see of them the better. But there are numerous prints on the sand near the water, and probably large numbers of them are in the habit of coming to this pool to drink. I expect therefore that we shall have a stirring night."

As soon as the oxen were unyoked, they were driven a short distance out to pasture. Five or six of the natives looked after them, while the remainder set to work to gather sticks and dried wood for the fires.

"I think," Tom said, "that I will go and have a bathe in the pool."

"You will do no such thing," Mr. Harvey remarked; "the chances are that there are half a dozen alligators in that pool—it is just the sort of place in which they lurk, for they find no difficulty in occasionally taking a deer or a wild hog, as he comes down to quench his thirst. There! don't you see something projecting above the water on the other side of the pool?"

"I see a bit of rough wood, that looks as if it were the top of a log underneath the water."

"Well, just watch it," Mr. Harvey said, as he took aim with his rifle.

He fired; the water instantly heaved and whirled at the spot the boy was watching; the supposed log rose higher out of the water, and then plunged down again; five or six feet of a long tail lashed the water and then disappeared, but the eddies on the surface showed that there was a violent agitation going on underneath it.

"What do you think of your log now?" Mr. Harvey asked, smiling.

"Why, it was an alligator," Tom said. "Who would

have thought it?—it looked just like a bit of an old tree."

"What you saw," Mr. Harvey said, "was a portion of the head; the alligator often lies with just his eyes and nostrils out of water."

"Did you kill it, sir, do you think?" Dick asked.

"Oh! no," Mr. Harvey replied; "the ball would glance off his head, as it would from the side of an ironclad ship. It woke him up, and flustrated him a bit; but he is none the worse for it. So you see, Tom, that pool is hardly fit to bathe in."

"No, indeed, sir," Tom answered, turning a little pale at the thought of the danger which he had proposed to incur. "I would rather fight half a dozen lions than get into the water with those brutes."

"I don't know about half a dozen lions," Mr. Harvey said; "although certainly one lion is an easier foe to tackle than an alligator. But one can never be too careful about bathing in this country. In the smallest pools, only a few yards long and a few feet wide, an alligator may be lurking, especially if the weather is dry and the pools far apart. Even when only drawing water at such places it is well to be careful, and it is always the best plan to poke the bottom for a short distance round with a pole before dipping in a bucket. Remember, if you should ever happen to be seized by one of these animals, there is but one chance, and that is to turn at once and stick your thumbs into his eyes. It requires nerve when a brute has got you by the leg, but it is your only chance, and the natives, when seized by alligators, often escape by blinding their foes. The pain and sudden loss of sight always induces them to loose their hold."

"I hope I shall never have to try," Tom said, shivering.

"It is safer not, certainly," Mr. Harvey agreed; "but there, I see dinner is ready, and Jumbo has got a bucket of water, so you can douse your heads and wash your hands without fear of alligators."

At nightfall the cattle were all driven in. The horses and a few of the most valuable oxen were placed in the laager formed by the waggons; the rest were fastened outside to them, side by side, by their horns; at each corner the natives had piled up a great heap of firewood. An hour after sunset the roar of a lion was heard out on the plain; it was answered simultaneously in six .or eight directions, and the stamping of the oxen announced that the animals were conscious of danger.

"There are a troop of them about," Mr. Harvey said, "just as I feared. Put a little more wood on the fires, boys; it is as well to keep them burning briskly, but it will probably be some hours before they work themselves up to make an attack upon us."

As the time went on, the roaring became louder and more continuous.

"There must be a score of them at least," Mr. Harvey said; "they are ranging round and round the camp; they don't like the look of the fires."

By ten o'clock the roaring had approached so closely that Mr. Harvey thought that it was time to prepare for the defence; he took post at one side of the square, and placed the boys and Jumbo at the other three; Tony and the other hunter were to keep outside the cattle, and walk round and round. The armed natives were scattered round the square. The drivers and cattle-men were to move about among the animals, and do their best to pacify them, for already a perfect panic had seized upon the draught-cattle, and with starting eyes and coats ruffled by fear they were tugging and straining at their ropes.

"Quiet, you silly beasts," Dick said, leaning out of the waggon in which he had taken his place; "you are safer where you are than you would be anywhere else. If you got away and bolted out into the plain, as you want to do, you would be pulled down and killed in no time."

The fires were now blazing brightly, throwing a wide circle of light round the camp and making visible every object within fifty yards.

It had been arranged that so long as the lions kept at a distance and only approached singly the defenders of the various faces of the square should retain their positions; but that, should a formidable attack be made upon any one side, the white men with two of the natives with them should hasten to the point attacked.

Several times, as Dick stood in the waggon, rifle in

hand, straining his eyes at the darkness, he fancied he saw indistinct shadowy forms moving at the edge of the circle of light. Two or three times he raised his rifle to take aim, but the objects were so indistinct that he doubted whether his fancy had not deceived him.

Presently the crack of Mr. Harvey's rifle was heard, followed by a roar of a sharper and more angry nature than those which had preceded it. As if a signal had been given, three or four creatures came with great bounds out of the darkness towards the side where Dick was posted. Taking a steady aim, he fired. Tony, who was outside with the cattle on that side of the square, did the same. The other natives had been ordered to retain their fire until the lions were close enough to ensure each shot telling. The lion at which Dick had aimed paused for a moment with a terrific roar, and then bounded forward again. When he came within twenty yards of the oxen, the four natives posted by Dick's side fired. The lion for a moment fell ; then, gathering itself together, it sprang on to the back of a bullock, just in front of where Dick was standing. The lad had a second rifle in readiness, and leaning forward he placed the muzzle within two yards of the lion's head and fired. The animal rolled off the back of the bullock, who, with the one standing next to him, at once began to kick at it, endeavouring to get their heads round to gore it with their horns. The lion, however, lay unmoved ; Dick's last shot had been fatal.

M 264

"THE CONTINUOUS ROARING SHOWED THAT THE LIONS
WERE STILL CLOSE AT HAND."

The other lions on this side had bounded back into the darkness. From the other sides of the square the sound of firing proclaimed that similar attacks had been made ; but, as there was no summons for aid, Dick supposed that the attacks were isolated ones, and so, after recharging his rifles, he remained quietly at his post.

For some hours the attack was not renewed, though the continuous roaring showed that the lions were still close at hand. Mr. Harvey went round and advised the boys to lie down at their posts and get a little sleep, as the natives would keep watch.

"I don't think we have done with them yet," he said ; "we have killed three, but I think, by the roaring, the number has considerably increased within the last hour. It is probable that an attack will be made an hour or so before daybreak, and I expect it will be in earnest next time."

Dick accordingly lay down to sleep, but he was too excited to close his eyes.

After a long time it seemed to him that the roaring was dying away, and a drowsiness was stealing over him, when suddenly Mr. Harvey's rifle was heard and he shouted,—

"To this side—quick ! they are upon us."

Dick, Tom, and Jumbo, with the six natives, leapt from the waggons, and, running across the little enclosure, scrambled up into those on the other side. There was a momentary silence here, the whole of the defendants having discharged their pieces, and a number of lions bounding across the open were already close to the cattle.

The new-comers at once opened fire. Two or three of the lions sprang among the cattle; but the rest, intimidated by the noise and flash of the guns, and by the yelling and shouting of the natives, turned and made off again. Those among the cattle were soon disposed of, but not before they had killed three of the draught-oxen and seriously torn two others.

The roaring continued until daybreak, gradually, however, growing fainter and more distant, and it was evident that the attack had ceased.

" Are their skins worth anything ? " Dick asked.

" Yes, they are worth a few dollars apiece, except in the case of old lions, who are apt to become mangy, and these are not worth skinning. We have killed eight of them, but their skins will not be worth anything like so much as the cattle they have killed; however, it is well that it is no worse. An attack by these troops of lions is no joke; they are by far the most formidable animals of South Africa. I don't say that an attack by a herd of wild elephants would not be more serious, but I never heard of such a thing taking place. They are timid creatures, and easily scared, and except in the case of wounded animals or of solitary bulls they can scarcely be considered as dangerous."

When day broke, the natives set to work to skin the lions, with the exception of one whose skin was valueless. As soon as the operation was completed, the skins were packed in the waggons, the oxen were inspanned, and the caravan proceeded on its way, all being glad to leave so dangerous a locality.

The next evening they encamped upon a river, and the night passed without interruption. The following morning, just as they were about to start, Tony, who with the other hunters had gone out at daybreak, returned with the news that he had found the spoor of elephants, and that he believed a herd had passed along only a few hours before.

Mr. Harvey at once decided to halt where he was for another day. The oxen were again unyoked, and six of the armed natives having been left to guard the camp, under the direction of Jumbo, the whole of the rest, with the white men, set off in pursuit of the elephants.

The spoor was quite distinct, and even had this failed, there would have been no difficulty in following the track, for there were scattered here and there trees, and the elephants in passing had broken off many boughs, which, stripped of their leaves, lay upon the ground they had traversed.

Tony and the other hunter, whose name was Blacking, a sobriquet gained from the extreme swarthiness of his skin, scouted ahead, and presently held up their hands to those following them to advance quietly. The trees were very thick here, and Mr. Harvey and the boys dismounted and led their horses to the spot where the hunters had halted. They were standing at the edge of a large circular clearing, three quarters of a mile in diameter ; it had probably at one time been the site of a native village, for there were signs of cultivation, and a number of scattered heads of maize rose here and there, the descendants of a bygone mealy plantation. Feeding upon these were a herd of some twenty elephants ; of these the greater portion were females or young ones, but there were three fine males—one, a beast of unusual size.

"That is the master of the herd," Mr. Harvey said, "a savage-looking old customer ; he has a splendid pair of tusks, although the tip of one," he added, gazing at the elephant through his field-glass, "is broken off. I think that for the present we will leave him alone, and direct our attention to the other two males. I will take Tom and Jumbo with me ; you, Dick, shall have Tony and Blacking. Three of the natives shall go with each party, but you must not rely upon them much ; and, remember, the one fatal spot is the forehead. Fasten your horses up here, and leave two of the natives in charge. Let the other six go round to the opposite side of the clearing and advance slowly from that direction, showing themselves occasionally, so as to draw the attention of the herd towards them. The elephants will probably move leisurely in this direction. Take your station behind trees, moving your position carefully as they approach, so as to place yourselves as near as possible in the line of the elephant you have fixed on. We will take up our station a hundred yards to the right of where we are standing; do you go as far to the left. The natives will take the horses into a thicket some distance in the rear. Whichever of the two young male elephants comes nearest to you is your mark, ours is the other. If they keep near each other, we shall probably meet again here."

The two parties moved off to the places assigned to them, and the natives whose duty it was to drive the elephants started to their positions. Keeping some little distance back among the trees, so that they could observe the movements of the elephants, while themselves unseen, Dick and his party moved to the spot indicated, and then sat down.

For three quarters of an hour the elephants continued to feed upon the heads of maize; then the big male suddenly wheeled round, extended his great ears, lifted his trunk, and trumpeted. At this signal the others all gathered together, and stood gazing in the direction from which danger threatened. Again the old bull gave an angry scream. The others moved slowly away from the danger, but he advanced in the direction in which he had seen the natives.

"Very bad elephant that," Tony whispered to Dick; "he give heaps of trouble; you see him charge."

A minute or two later the elephant, catching sight of his enemies, quickened his pace, and with his little tail switching angrily, uplifted trunk, and widespread ears, he charged down upon them at a pace of which Dick had not supposed so cumbersome a beast would be capable.

In a moment the distant natives were seen to rise from the grass and to run at full speed back towards the wood. The elephant pursued them until he reached the trees; here he halted, and gazed for some time into the wood. Then seeing no signs of the natives—for these knew better than to provoke so vicious a beast by firing at him—he trumpeted defiantly, and slowly retraced his steps towards the rest of the herd. These, led by the two males, were already approaching the trees behind which Dick and his party were lying concealed. Before they had arrived here Mr. Harvey and his party came up.

Dick and Tom were both carrying heavy smooth-bore guns, similar to those used by the Boers. These their fathers had purchased at Newcastle on the day of their start; they were old weapons, but very strong and serviceable; they carried a heavy charge of powder and a large ball, of a mixture of lead and tin, specially made for elephant-shooting.

"Dick fire first," Blacking whispered in his ear; "if he not kill him, then the rest of us fire."

Dick was lying down behind the trunk of a tree, his rifle steadied against it; when the elephant was within a distance of twenty yards he fired, taking steady aim at the vital point. The recoil of the piece was tremendous, and the roar of its report almost stunned him; he gave, however, a shout of delight, for the elephant stood for half a minute swaying

M 264

"DICK FIRED INTO THE ELEPHANT'S OPEN MOUTH, AND THEN
LEAPT BEHIND THE TREE."

from side to side, and then fell heavily upon the ground.

Mr. Harvey had given Tom the first shot at the other elephant; but, just at the moment when the lad was about to fire, the elephant gave a sudden start at the report of Dick's rifle, and Tom's shot struck it at the side of the head and glancing off passed through its ear. Throwing up its trunk, the elephant instantly charged. Mr. Harvey fired, but the uplifted trunk prevented his getting an accurate aim at the vital spot. The bullet passed through the trunk, and then glanced off the forehead. The elephant swerved and showed its side, at which a general volley was fired by all the guns still loaded. The great beast stood still for an instant, stumbled forward a few strides, and then its legs seemed to bend beneath it, and it sank down quietly to the ground.

Just at this moment, as the affrighted cows were turning to fly across the plain, there was a thundering rush, and the great elephant charged through them, and passing between the dead males dashed into the wood. Its rush was so sudden and headlong that it carried the elephant past the men standing behind the trees; but it speedily checked itself, and turning round made a rush upon them. There was an instant stampede. Most of the natives at once threw away their guns; some climbed hastily up into the trees against which they were standing; others took to the bushes. The elephant charged in after these, but seeing no signs of them he speedily came out again and looked round for a fresh foe. His eye fell upon Dick, who had just recharged his rifle.

"Run, Dick! run!" shouted Mr. Harvey.

But Dick saw that the elephant was upon him, while the tree near which he was standing was too thick to climb. The elephant was holding his head so high that Dick could not aim at the spot on the forehead, but, waiting until the animal was within ten yards of him, he fired into its open mouth, and then leapt behind the tree. With a scream of pain the elephant rushed on, but being unable to check himself he came full butt with tremendous force against the tree, which quivered under the blow, and Dick, thinking that it was going to fall upon him, sprang back a pace. Three or four more shots were fired before the elephant could turn, and then wheeling round it charged upon its new assailants.

Tom was one of those nearest to him ; the boy had just discharged his rifle and advanced a few feet from the tree behind which he had been standing. Before he could regain it he felt something pass round him, there was a tremendous squeeze, which stopped his breath and seemed to press his life out of him, then he felt himself flying high into the air, and became insensible.

Apparently satisfied with what he had done, the elephant continued his rapid pace into the open again, and followed the retreating herd across the plain.

Dick had given a cry of horror, as he saw the elephant seize his friend, and his heart seemed to stand still when he saw him whirled high in the air. Tom fell into a thick and bushy tree, and there, breaking through the light foliage at the top, remained suspended in the upper boughs.

In an instant Jumbo climbed the tree, and making his way to the lad lifted him from the fork in which he was wedged, placed him on his shoulder as easily as if he had been a child, and descending the tree laid him on the ground by the side of Mr. Harvey. The latter at once knelt beside him.

"Thank God, he is breathing!" he exclaimed at once. "Lift his head, Dick; open his shirt, Blacking; and give me some water out of your gourd. I trust he is only stunned; that brute was in such a hurry that he had not time to squeeze him fairly, and the tree has broken his fall. If he had come down to the ground from that height, it must have killed him."

He sprinkled some water upon the lad's face and chest, and to his and Dick's delight Tom presently opened his eyes. He looked round in a surprised and half-stupid way, and then made an effort to rise, but a cry broke from him as he did so.

"Lie still, Tom," Mr. Harvey said; "you are hurt, but, I hope, not severely. Cut his shirt off, Dick; I expect some of his ribs are broken."

Upon Mr. Harvey carefully feeling Tom's ribs, he found, as he had expected, that five of them were broken—three on one side and two on the other.

"Some of your ribs are damaged, Tom," he said
cheerfully; "but that is of no great consequence;
they all seem pretty fairly in their places. Now I will
bandage you tightly, so as to keep them there, and
then we will carry you back to the waggons and nurse
you until they grow together again; young bones
soon heal, and in a week or ten days you will, I hope,
be able to travel again; you had a close shave of it.
I never met a more savage beast than that bull-
elephant in all my experience."

CHAPTER XII.

AN ATTACK BY ELEPHANTS.

A LITTER was speedily constructed from some boughs of trees, and Tom being placed in it was at once carried back to the camp, escorted by his friend. The hunters remained behind to cut out the tusks of the two elephants that had fallen. A portion of the trunks and feet, which are considered the most delicate portions of the elephant, was laid aside for the use of the white men, and a large quantity of meat was brought back to camp for the natives.

The sound of firing had brought up some people from a small village two or three miles away, and these to their immense joy were allowed to carry off enough meat to enable them to feast to the utmost extent of their ability for a week to come.

Mr. Harvey had in the course of his wanderings frequently had occasion to dress wounds and bandage broken bones; he was therefore able to apply the necessary bandages to Tom, and the lad was soon lying in comparative ease on a bed formed of rags Generally the boys slept in hammocks, but Mr. Harvey insisted that Tom must lie perfectly straight on his back until the bones had begun to set again.

"We made a sad mess with that old bull to-day, Dick," he said. "It is humiliating to think that he should have charged us all, injured Tom, and got away almost unscathed."

"You see, sir," Dick said, "he attacked us unexpectedly; our guns were all discharged, and he came on with such a rush that there was no getting a steady shot at him. The whole affair lasted little more than a minute, I should say."

"I shall go out to-morrow morning," Mr. Harvey said, "and take up the track again, and see if I cannot get even with the beast. There is time enough to-day, for it is still early, but the herd will be so restless and suspicious that there will be no getting near them, and I should not care to face that old bull unless I had a fair chance of killing him at the first shot. He has a magnificent pair of tusks, and ivory sells so high that they would be worth a good deal of trouble and some risk to get."

"Shall I go with you, sir?"

"No, Dick, I would rather you did not. The business will be more dangerous than usual, and I should not like the responsibility of having you with me. Tom had as narrow a shave yesterday as ever I saw, and I certainly do not want two of you on my hands."

Dick was not sorry at Mr. Harvey's decision, for after the charge of the bull-elephant he felt just at present he should not care about encountering another. The next morning Mr. Harvey, accompanied by the three native hunters and the greater portion of the others, started in pursuit of the elephants.

Dick, after sitting for some time with Tom, took his gun and wandered round near the camp, shooting birds. As the sun got high, and the heat became fiercer and fiercer, he returned to camp, and had just taken off his coat and sat down by the side of Tom when he heard shouts of terror outside the tent.

Running out to see what was the matter, he saw the natives in a state of wild terror. They pointed across the plain, and Dick, to his astonishment and alarm, saw a great elephant approaching at a rapid trot, with his trunk in the air and his ears extended to the fullest. He recognized at once the bull which had charged them on the previous day. The natives were now flying in all directions. Dick shouted to them to stand and get their muskets, but his words were unheeded; he ran to the tent, seized the long-bore gun which he had carried the day before and also that of Tom, and charged them both hastily, but coolly.

"What on earth is it all about?" Tom asked.

"It is the elephant again, Tom; lie quiet, whatever you do; you cannot run away, so lie just as you are."

Then with a gun in each hand Dick ran out of the tent again. The elephant was now but a hundred yards away. Dick climbed into a waggon standing in the line on which he was coming, knelt down in the bottom and rested the muzzle on the side, standing up and waving his arm before he did so, so as to attract the attention of the elephant. The great beast saw him,

and trumpeting loudly came straight down at him ;
Dick knelt, as steady as a rock, with the sight of the
gun upon the elephant's forehead.

When he was within twenty yards Dick drew the
trigger, and, without waiting to see the result, snatched
up and levelled the second gun. The elephant had
staggered as he was hit, and then, as with a great effort,
he pulled himself together and again moved forward,
but with a stumbling and hesitating step ; taking
steady aim again, Dick fired when the elephant's trunk
was within a yard of the muzzle of his gun, and then
springing to his feet, leapt on the opposite side of the
waggon and took to his heels.

After running a few steps, he glanced back over
his shoulder, and then ceased running ; the elephant
was no longer in sight above the waggon, but had
fallen an inert mass by its side.

"All right, Tom !" Dick shouted loudly ; "I have
done for him."

Before going to look at the fallen elephant Dick
went to the spot where stood the piled muskets of the
natives who had fled ; dropping a ramrod into
them, he found that two were loaded, and taking
these in his hands he advanced towards the elephant.
The precaution was needless ; the great beast lay
dead ; the two heavy balls had struck within an inch
or two of each other, and penetrated the brain. The
first would have been fatal, and the elephant
was about to fall when Dick had fired the second
time.

Gradually the drivers and other natives returned to camp with shouts of triumph. These, however, Dick speedily silenced by a volley of abuse for their cowardice in running away and leaving Tom to his fate. A few minutes later Mr. Harvey galloped in at full speed, closely followed by the swift-footed Blacking.

"Thank God, you are safe, my boys," Mr. Harvey said, as he leapt from his horse. "I have had a terrible fright. We followed the spoor to the point where they had passed the night ; here the trackers were much puzzled by the fact that the great elephant, whose tracks were easily distinguished from the others, seemed to have passed the night in rushing furiously about. Numbers of young trees had been torn up by the roots, and great branches twisted off the larger trees. They concluded that he must have received some wound which had maddened him with pain. We took up the track where the herd had moved on, but soon found that he had separated himself from it, and had gone off at full speed by himself. We set off in pursuit, observing a good deal of caution, for if he had turned, as was likely enough, and had come upon us while in such a frantic state, we should have had to bolt for our lives. I was thinking only of this when I saw the hunters talking together and gesticulating. I soon found out what was the matter. They told me that if the elephant kept on in the line he was taking, it would assuredly bring him in sight of the camp. if not straight upon it. As I had no doubt that he would in that case attack it, I put spurs to my horse at once, and dashed on at full speed in hopes of overtaking the elephant, and turning it, before it came within sight of the camp. I became more and more anxious as I neared the camp and found the elephant was still before me; then I heard two shots close together, and I could hear no others, and you may guess how relieved I was when I caught sight of the camp, and saw the natives gathered round something which was, I had no doubt, the elephant. I had feared that I should see the whole place in confusion, the waggons upset, and above all the tent levelled. Thank God, my dear boy, you are all safe! Now tell me all about it."

Dick related the circumstances, and Mr. Harvey praised him highly for the promptness, coolness, and courage with which he had acted. Then he roundly abused the natives in their own language for their cowardly conduct.

"Are you not ashamed of yourselves?" he asked; "what do you carry your arms for, if you are afraid to use them? Here are sixteen men, all with muskets, who run away in a panic, and leave one white lad to defend his wounded friend alone."

The reproaches of Mr. Harvey were mild by the side of the abuse which the three hunters—for by this time Tony and Jumbo had reached the camp—lavished upon their compatriots.

"What are you good for?" they asked scornfully; "you are fit only to be slaves to the Dutch; the master had better hire women to march with him; he ought to take your arms away, and to set you to spin."

Crestfallen as the natives were at their own cowardice, they were roused by the abuse of the hunters, and a furious quarrel would have ensued, had not Mr. Harvey interposed his authority and smoothed matters down, admitting that the attack of the enraged elephant was really terrifying, and telling the natives that now they saw how well the white men could fight, they would no doubt be ready to stand by them next time.

The hunters now proceeded to cut out the tusks of the elephant. When they did so the cause of the animal's singular behaviour became manifest; a ball had struck him just at the root of the tusk, and had buried itself in one of the nerves there, no doubt causing excruciating pain.

The tusks were grand ones, Mr. Harvey saying that he had seldom seen a finer pair. The news of the slaughter of three elephants drew together a considerable number of natives, who were delighted to receive permission to carry off as much meat as they chose. When the greater portion of the flesh of the old bull had been removed, ten oxen were harnessed to the remains of the carcass, and it was dragged to a distance from camp, as Mr. Harvey was desirous of remaining where he was for some days longer on Tom's account, and the effluvia from the carcass would in a very short time have rendered the camp uninhabitable had it remained in the vicinity.

In a week Tom was convalescent ; he was still, however, very stiff and sore. A hammock was therefore slung under the tilt of one of the waggons, the sides were drawn up to allow of a free passage of air, and the caravan then went forward on its journey.

For the next fortnight nothing of importance happened ; sometimes the journeys were short, sometimes extremely long, being regulated entirely by the occurrence of water. At many of the halting-places a good deal of trade was done, as the news of the coming of the caravan spread far ahead of it, and the natives for a considerable distance on each side of the line of route came down to trade with it. They brought with them skins of beasts and birds, small packets of gold-dust, ostrich feathers, and occasionally ivory. Mr. Harvey was well content with his success so far.

For some time past, owing to the disturbed state of the country and the demand for waggons occasioned by the war, the number of traders who had made their way north had been very small, and the natives consequently were eager to buy cotton and cloth, and to get rid of the articles which they had been accumulating for the purpose of barter with the whites. Never before, Mr. Harvey said, had he done so good a trade in so short a time.

At the end of the fortnight after starting Tom was again able to take his seat in the saddle and ride quietly along by the side of the caravan, Mr. Harvey warning him on no account to go above a walking pace at present, as a jerk or a jar might break the newly-knit bones, and undo all the work that had been effected.

In the meantime Dick, accompanied by one or other of the hunters, always rode out from the line of march, and had no difficulty in providing an ample supply of game. He was careful, however, not to shoot more than was required, for both he and Mr. Harvey viewed with abhorrence the taking of life unnecessarily, merely for the purpose of sport. He was able, nevertheless, to kill a great many deer without feeling that their flesh was wasted; for not only were the number of mouths in the caravan large, and their powers of eating wonderful, but the natives who came in to trade were always glad to eat up any surplus that remained—and indeed Mr. Harvey found the liberal distribution of meat opened their hearts and much facilitated trade.

Two or three days after they had left the scene of the elephant-hunt some objects were seen far out on the plain, which the hunters at once pronounced to be ostriches. Dick would have started in pursuit, but Mr. Harvey checked him.

"They can run," he said, "faster than a horse can gallop. They can indeed be ridden down, as they almost always run in a great circle, and the pursuit can be taken up with fresh horses, but this is a long business. We will send the hunters out first, to get on the other side of them, and when they are posted we will ride out. Going quite slowly the attention of the birds will be directed to us ; this will give the hunters an opportunity of creeping up on the other side and shooting or lassoing them. If I am not mistaken they have a good many young ones with them—this is about the time of year when this is usually the case. If we could catch a dozen of them, they would be prizes, for they fetch a good sum down in the colony, where ostrich-farming is carried on on a large scale. They are very easily tamed, and would soon keep with the caravan and give no trouble."

After remaining quiet for some little time, to give the hunters time to make a wide circuit, Mr. Harvey and Dick rode quietly forward towards the birds, who stood on a slight swell of ground at a distance of about half a mile, evidently watching the caravan with great interest.

By Mr. Harvey's instructions Dick unrolled the blanket which he always carried on his saddle, and taking an end in each hand held it out at arm's length on a level with the top of his head, Mr. Harvey doing the same.

"They are silly birds," Mr. Harvey said, "and their attention is easily caught by anything they don't understand. Like all other wild creatures they are afraid of man ; but by holding the blankets out like sails they do not see our outline, and cannot make out what the strange creatures advancing towards them can be."

At a foot-pace they advanced towards the ostriches ; these made no signs of retreat until the horsemen approached to within about seventy yards. Then from the brow behind the birds the three hunters suddenly rose up, and whirling the balls of their lassoes round their heads launched them among the ostriches. Three birds fell with the cords twisted round their legs, and two more were shot as the startled flock dashed off at full speed across the plain. Mr. Harvey and Dick dropped their blankets, and started at full gallop.

" Bring down an old bird if you can, Dick, and then let the rest go, and give your attention to cutting off the young ones."

Dick fired at one of the old birds, but missed ; Mr. Harvey brought one to the ground. The young ostriches, which were but a few weeks old, soon began to tail off in the race, and after ten minutes' riding Mr. Harvey and Dick had the satisfaction of getting ahead of them and turning them. A little more driving brought the frightened creatures to a stand-still, and most of them dropped in a squatting position to the ground, huddled together like frightened chickens. They were sixteen in number, but one which had fallen and broken its leg was at once shot. The legs of the young ostrich are extremely brittle, and one of the troubles of the farmers who rear them is that they so frequently break their bones and have to be killed.

Blacking was sent off at his best speed to overtake the caravan and bring back a dozen men with him. The ostriches which had been lassoed had been at once killed by the hunters, and the feathers of the five killed by them and of that shot by Mr. Harvey were pulled out. Three out of the six were in splendid plumage.

"How much are each of those feathers worth?" Dick asked.

" Those fine white ones will fetch from 1*l.* to 1*l.* 5*s.* apiece out here—some as high as 30*s.* A perfect ostrich feather, fit for a court-plume, will sell in England for 3*l.* to 5*l.* The small, dark-coloured feathers are worth from sixpence to one shilling apiece."

The young birds, after their wings had been tied to their sides, were lifted and carried away, Dick being unable to help laughing at their long legs sticking out in front of the bearers, and at their long necks and beaks, with which from time to time they inflicted sharp pecks on the men who were carrying them.

When the caravan was overtaken, the birds were placed in a waggon, and in the evening were liberated inside the laager formed by the waggons. Some grain was thrown to them, and they soon began to pick this up. After this their expression was rather one of curiosity than fear, and they exhibited no alarm whatever when Dick, scattering some more corn, came in and moved quietly among them. For the first few days they were carried in a waggon, but at the end of that time they were completely domesticated. After the camp was formed they walked about, like barn-door fowls, picking up any scraps of food that were thrown to them, and indeed getting so bold as some-

times to attempt to snatch it from the men's hands.
When on the march, they stalked gravely along by the
side of the waggons.

"What is the value of an ostrich?" Dick asked Mr.
Harvey one day.

"An ostrich of about three or four months old,"
Mr. Harvey replied, "is worth from 30*l.* to 50*l.* A
full-grown cock and two hens, the stock with which
most small settlers begin ostrich-farming, are worth
from 200*l.* to 400*l.* Each hen will lay about fifty
eggs in a year, so that if only half are reared and
sold at the rate of 20*l.* apiece, which is a low price, at
three weeks old, there is a good profit upon them.
The young birds increase in value at the rate of about
3*l.* per month. The feathers are generally sold by
weight; fine plumes go from seventy to ninety to the
pound, and fetch from 40*l.* to 50*l.* The feathers of the
wild birds are worth a third more than those of the tame
ones, as they are stronger. The quantity of feathers
sold is astonishing. One firm in Port Elizabeth often
buys 10,000 pounds' weight of ostrich feathers per
week. Of course these are not all first-class plumes,
and the prices range down as low as 3*l.* or 50*s.* for the
poorest kind."

"Where do they get water out here in the desert?"

"They have no difficulty here," Mr. Harvey replied,
"for an ostrich thinks nothing of going twenty or
thirty miles; but they require to drink very seldom."

"How many feathers can be plucked from each
bird a year?"

"About three quarters of a pound of first-class feathers, besides the inferior sorts. There are now such quantities of ostriches in the colony, that the price of feathers has gone down materially, and is now not so high as the figures I have given you. The highest class feathers, however, still maintain their price, and are likely to do so, for the demand for feathers in Europe increases at as rapid a rate as does the production."

"I suppose they could not be kept in England?" Dick asked; "for there must be a splendid profit on such farming."

"No," Mr. Harvey replied; "they want above all things a dry climate. Warmth is of course important, but even this is less essential than dryness. They may be reared in England under artificial conditions, but they would never grow up strong and healthy in this way, and would no doubt be liable to disease—besides, as even in their native country you see that the feathers deteriorate in strength and diminish in value in domesticated birds, there would probably be so great a falling off in the yield and value of feathers in birds kept under artificial conditions in England that the speculation would not be likely to pay."

"Do the hens sit on their eggs, as ordinary hens?"

"Just the same," Mr. Harvey answered, "and very funny they look with their long legs sticking out. Not only does the hen sit, but the cock takes his turn at keeping the eggs warm when the mother goes out to feed."

"I shall ask father," Dick said, "when we get back, to arrange to take these fifteen ostriches as part of his share of the venture; it would be great fun to see them stalking about."

"Ah! we have not got them home yet," Mr. Harvey replied, smiling; "we must not be too sanguine. We have certainly begun capitally, but there is no saying what adventures are before us yet. We have been particularly fortunate in seeing nothing of the tzetze fly. As you know, we have made several considerable détours to avoid tracts of country where they are known to prevail, still, occasionally they are met with in unexpected places, and I have seldom made a trip without losing some of my horses and cattle from them."

"How is it that a fly can kill a horse? They are not larger than our blue-bottles at home, for I saw one in a naturalist's window in Pieter-Maritzburg."

"It is a mystery, Dick, which has not yet been solved; there are flies in other parts of the world, whose bite is sufficiently poisonous to raise bumps underneath the skins of animals, but nothing approaching the tzetze in virulence. It certainly appears unaccountable that the venom of so small a creature should be able to kill a great animal like a horse or an ox."

"Is it found only in the south of Africa?"

"No, Dick, it extends more or less over the whole

of the plateau-lands of Africa, and is almost as great a scourge in the highlands of Egypt as it is here."

"I wonder," Dick said thoughtfully, "why the tzetze was created; most insects are useful as scavengers, or to furnish food for birds, but I cannot see the use of a fly which is so terribly destructive as this."

"I can't tell you, my boy," Mr. Harvey said. "That everything, even the tzetze has a good purpose, you may be sure, even though it is hidden from us. Possibly, for example, it may be discovered some day that the tzetze is an invaluable medicine for some disease to which man is subject, just as blistering powder is obtained from the crest-body of the cantharides beetle. However, we must be content to take it on trust. We must leave our descendants something to discover, you know, Dick; for if we go on inventing and discovering as we are doing, it is clear that they must look out for fresh channels for research."

CHAPTER XIII.

A BRUSH WITH THE NATIVES.

ONE day Jumbo touched Dick's arm, as he was riding along with the caravan, and, pointing to a clump of trees at some little distance, said,—

"Giraffe."

Dick reined in his horse, and gazed at the trees.

"I don't see it," he said.

"They are very difficult to see," Mr. Harvey re-marked; "they have a knack somehow of standing so as to look like a part of the tree. I don't see him myself, but if Jumbo says he is there, you may be sure he is."

"Is the skin valuable?" Dick asked.

"No, Dick, it would not be worth cumbering ourselves with. Nor is the flesh very good to eat—I do not say it cannot be eaten, but we have plenty of venison. I never like shooting a giraffe when I can help it. Clumsy and awkward as they are, they have wonderfully soft and expressive eyes, and I do not know anything more piteous than the look of a dying giraffe; however, if you ride up to the trees and set them scampering, you will get a good laugh, for their run is as awkward and clumsy as that of any living creature."

Dick accordingly started at a gallop towards the

trees ; it was not until he was close to them that he saw three giraffes, two old ones and a young one. They started off, as he approached, at a pace which seemed to Dick to be slow, as well as extraordinarily clumsy. The two old ones kept themselves between their offspring and the pursuer, as if to shield it from a shot. Dick, however, had no idea of firing; he only wished to gallop up close, so as to get a nearer view of these singular beasts, but to his astonishment he found that, although his horse was going at its best speed, the apparently slow-moving giraffes were steadily gaining upon him. He could hardly at first believe his eyes. But he was gradually tailed off, and at last, reining in his horse, he sat in the saddle and enjoyed a good laugh at the strange trio in front of him, with their long, straggling legs and necks.

When he rejoined the caravan Mr. Harvey, who had watched the pursuit, asked him laughingly if he managed to catch the giraffe.

"I might as soon have tried to catch an express train ; they went right away from me,—and Tommy can gallop too ; but he hadn't a chance with them, although he did his best."

"They do move along at a tremendous pace in their clumsy fashion. They take such immense strides with those odd long legs of theirs, that one has no idea of their speed until one chases them. I never knew a new hand who tried it, but he was sure to come back with a crestfallen face."

Three weeks after leaving what they called the

elephant-camp the caravan halted for two days. They had now arrived at the spot where their troubles with the natives might be expected to begin; they were at the border of the Matabele country, and here Mr. Harvey intended to turn west, and after keeping along for some time to bend to the south and re-enter the colony north of Kimberley, and to journey down to Port Elizabeth, which is the principal mart for goods from the interior. Between the Matabele and the tribes on their border hostilities had for some time prevailed, and while they halted Mr. Harvey sent forward Blacking with a few presents to the chief of the next tribe, saying that he was coming through his country to trade, and asking for a promise that he should not be interfered with in his passage.

At the end of the second day the messenger returned.

"The chief says come; he says he has been a long time without trade. But before he answered he talked with his chiefs, and I don't know whether he means honestly. The tribe has a bad name; they are thieves and robbers."

"Well, we will go on," Mr. Harvey said, "neverthe-less; we have got the chief's word, and he will not after that venture to attack us openly, for if he did he knows very well that no more traders would visit his country. His people may make attacks upon us, but we are strong enough to hold our own. We muster about thirty guns, and in our laager would be able to beat off his whole tribe, did they attack us; we will, however, while travelling through his country, be more careful than hitherto. The waggons shall, when it is possible, travel two abreast, so that the line will not be so long to guard, and you must not wander away to shoot. Fortunately we have a store of dried meat, which will last us for some time "

On the following morning the caravans set out, and after travelling twelve miles halted on the bank of a stream. Soon after they had formed their camp five or six natives came in; they brought a few bunches of ostrich plumes and some otter skins ; these they bartered for cotton, and having concluded their bargains wandered about in the camp, as was the custom of the natives, peeping into the waggons, examining the bullocks, and looking at all the arrangements with childish curiosity.

" I expect these fellows have come as spies rather than traders," Mr. Harvey said to the lads. " As a general thing the natives come in with their wives and children; but, you see, these are all men. I observed too that they have particularly examined the pile of muskets, as if reckoning up our means of defence. In future, instead of merely a couple of men to look after the cattle and keep off any marauders, I will put six every night on guard ; they shall be relieved twice during the night, and one of the hunters shall be in charge of each watch,—if there are signs of trouble, we will ourselves take it by turns."

Two or three times that night the sentries perceived moving objects near the camp, and challenged; in each case the objects at once disappeared; whether they were hyenas or crawling men could not be discerned.

At the halt next day a much larger number of natives came in, and a satisfactory amount of trade was done. Their demeanour, however, was insolent and overbearing, and some of them went away with their goods, declining to accept the exchange offered. After they had left the camp several small articles were missed.

The next day they passed across a plain abounding in game, and Mr. Harvey said that the boys and the three hunters might go out and kill some fresh meat; but he warned Dick and Tom not to allow their ardour in the chase to carry them away from the hunters, but to keep as much as possible together. When they had killed as many animals as could be carried on their horses and the hunters' shoulders, they were to return at once.

It was the first time that Tom had been out hunting since his accident; his bones had all set well, and beyond a little stiffness and occasional pain he was quite himself again.

"I am glad to be riding out again with you, Dick," he said; "it has been awfully slow work jogging along by the side of the caravan."

In addition to the three hunters they took as usual a native with them, to hold the horses should it be necessary to dismount and stalk the game, instead of chasing it and shooting it from the saddles, an

exercise in which by this time the boys were efficient.
They found more difficulty in getting up to the game
than they had expected, and the hunters said confidently that the animals must have been chased or
disturbed within a few hours. They had accordingly
to go four or five miles across the plain before they
could get a shot ; but at last they saw a herd feeding
in a valley. After the experience they had had that
morning of the futility of attempting to get near
the deer on horseback, they determined that the
hunters should make a circuit, and come down
upon the herd from different points. Tom and
Dick were to stay on the brow where they were
then standing, keeping well back, so as to be out
of sight from the valley, until they heard the report
of the first gun, when they were to mount and
endeavour to cut off and head the deer back upon
the others. The hunters then started—Jumbo and
Blacking going to the right, Tony and the other to
the left.

After an hour's walking they reached their places
at points about equidistant from each other, forming
with Tom and Dick a complete circle round the deer.
They were enabled to keep each other in sight,
although hidden from the herd in the hollow. When
each had gained his station they lay down and began
to crawl towards the deer, and until they were within
150 yards of the herd the latter continued grazing
quietly. Then an old buck gave a short, sharp cry, and
struck the ground violently with his hoofs; the others

all ceased feeding, and gazed with startled eyes to windward, and were about to dash off in a body when the four men fired almost simultaneously, and as many stags fell. The rest darted off at full speed in the direction in which Tom and Dick were posted, that being the only side open to them. An instant later Tom and Dick appeared on horseback on the brow, and dashed down towards the herd ; these, alarmed at the appearance of a fresh enemy, broke into two bodies, scattering right and left, giving both lads an opportunity for a good shot. Both succeeded in bringing down their mark. They then dismounted, and giving their horses to the native joined the hunters. They had bagged six deer, and the hunters at once proceeded to disembowel them ; one was to be slung behind each of the saddles, and the others would be carried by the hunters and native.

While they were so engaged they were startled by a shout, and saw the native running down towards them, leading the horses and gesticulating wildly.

"We are attacked," Blacking said, and almost at the same moment three or four arrows fell among them.

They had collected the dead deer at one spot, and were standing in a group ; looking round they saw a large number of natives crowning the low hills all round them, and saw that while they had been stalking the deer they themselves had been stalked by the natives. Without a moment's hesitation the hunters disposed the bodies of the deer in a circle ; seizing the two

horses they threw them beside the deer, fastening their
limbs with the lassoes which they carried, so that they
could not move ; then the six men threw themselves down in the circle.

All this had been done in a couple of minutes.
The arrows were falling fast among them, but none had
been hit, and as soon as the preparations were complete they opened a steady fire at the enemy. With
the exception of the man who had come out with
the horses all were good shots, and their steady fire
at once checked the advance of the natives, whose
triumphant yelling ceased, as man after man went
down, and they speedily followed the example of
their opponents, and, throwing themselves down on
the grass, kept up a fire with their arrows in a circle
of seventy or eighty yards round the hunters.

Gradually, however, their fire ceased, for to use
their bows they were obliged to show their heads
above the grass, and whenever one did so the sharp
crack of a rifle was heard; and so often did the bullets
fly true to their aim that the natives soon grew chary
of exposing themselves.

"What will they do now?" Dick asked, as the firing
ceased.

"They are cowards," Jumbo said contemptuously.
"If they had been Zulus, or Swazis, or Matabele, they
would have rushed in upon us, and finished it at
once."

"Well, I am very glad they are not," Dick said;
"but what is to be done?"

"They will wait for night," Tony answered; "then,

when we cannot see them, they will creep up close and charge."

"In that case," Dick said, "the best thing will be for us to keep in a body, and fight our way through them, and make for the camp."

Jumbo shook his head.

"They quiet now because they think they got us safe; if we try to get away, they rush down upon us; we shoot many, but we all get killed."

"Then," Dick said, "the best thing will be for me to jump on my horse and ride straight through them; if I get off alive, I will make for the caravan and bring back Mr. Harvey and the rest to your assistance."

"No good," Blacking said; "your horse would be stuck full of arrows before you get away; he drop dead; they kill you. I go."

"But it would be just as dangerous for you as for me, Blacking."

"No," the hunter said; "directly you stand up to get on horse they see you and get ready to shoot; the horse fall dead before he reach them. I will crawl through the grass; they will not see me till I get to them—perhaps I get through without them seeing at all; if not, I jump up sudden and run; they all surprised, no shoot straight; once through line they never catch me."

Jumbo and Tony assented with a grunt, and Dick, seeing that no better plan could be suggested, offered no opposition to the young hunter undertaking the task.

Leaving his gun and ammunition behind him, the

black at once without a word crawled out between
the carcases of the deer, making his way, like a snake,
perfectly flat on his stomach, and soon it was only by
a very slight movement of the grass, which was nearly
two feet high, that Dick could follow his progress.
But he could not do this for long, an arrow whizzing
close to his head warned him that he was exposing
himself, and he lay down behind his stag and listened
with intense eagerness for the outcry which would
arise when Blacking was discovered.

It seemed a long time, so slow and cautious
was the black's advance.   At last there was a
sudden yell, and the little party, sure that the
attention of their assailants would for the moment
be diverted, raised their heads from the shelter
and looked out.   They saw Blacking bounding
at full speed up the slope; a score of natives had
sprung to their feet, and were discharging their arrows
in the direction of the fugitive, who zigzagged, as he
ran with rapid bounds, to unsteady and divert their
aim. One arrow struck him in the side; they saw
him break off the feather-head, pull it through the
wound, and throw it away without a moment's pause
in his flight.

"Is it a serious wound?" Tom asked eagerly.

Jumbo shook his head.

"Not kill him," he said; "too near skin."

By this time Blacking's pursuers had thrown their
bows across their shoulders, and grasping their assegais
had started in pursuit.

M 264

"BLACKING BROKE OFF THE ARROW'S FEATHER-HEAD WITHOUT
PAUSE IN HIS FLIGHT."

" They no catch him," Tony said confidently; " Black-ing clever man ; he not run too fast ; let them keep close behind him ; they think they catch him, and keep on running all the way to camp. People here watch, not tink to attack us ; then they wait again for the oders to come back ; half of dem gone, a good many killed, they not like to attack us now."

"What do you say, Tony ?—shall we get up and follow in a body slowly ? "

" That would be good plan," Tony said, " if sure no more black men come ; but if others come and join dem, dey attack us out on plain, we got no stags to lie behind. Dey fight hard 'caus they know that Blacking have got away, and that help come ; make bad affair of it ; better stop here."

Presently two or three of the natives were seen coming back over the brow, having given up the pur-suit. Dick's rifle was a good one, and the brow was not more than 400 yards away ; he took a steady aim and fired, and one of the natives fell. A yell of astonishment broke from the others, and they threw themselves instantly on the grass. This, however, although long enough to shelter them in the bottom, was shorter and scantier on the slope. The inclined position too enabled Dick to see them, and he again fired. He could not see where the ball struck, but it must have been close to the two natives, for these leapt to their feet and bounded back again over the brow.

" That was a capital shot of yours, Dick," Tom said. " I will try next time. Our rifles will carry easily

enough as far as that, although the hunters' won't. If
we can but prevent any of these fellows who have
gone after Blacking from coming down and rejoining
those round us, we are safe enough, for if they did
not dare to make a rush when there were about sixty
of them they will not try now when there are not half
that number."

An hour later a party of some ten or twelve natives
appeared again on the brow. Dick and Tom at once
fired. One of them fell, and the rest again retired
behind the brow, shouting something to those below,
which Tony at once translated that Blacking had got
away. The news, added to the effect of the fall of their
comrades on the height, dispirited the natives below,
and one or two were to be seen stealing up the
slopes.

Dick and Tom were on the alert, and one of the
natives fell with a broken leg ; this completed the
uneasiness of the party below.   Creeping away from
the deadly rifles to the foot of the slopes, they suddenly
rose and bounded up it. A general volley was fired
by the beleaguered party, and two more natives fell ;
the rest dashed up the slope, two of them on the way
lifting and carrying off their wounded comrades.

" We all right now," Jumbo said ; " dey no attack us
here any more ; like enough dey wait and lie in ambush
in grass, in case we move away ; but we not do that ;
we sit here quietly till the caravan arrive."

. " Do you think Mr. Harvey will bring the whole
caravan ? "

" Sure to do dat," Jumbo said. " He no able to leave party to protect the waggons and to send party here to us; he bring the caravan all along together. If he attacked, he make laager; but me no tink dey attack. The people ready to cut off little party; den the chief say he not responsible, but if his people attack the caravan dat different thing."

The hours passed slowly; the heat in the bottom, as the sun, almost overhead, poured its rays down into it, was very great. As the hours passed on the heat became less oppressive, but it was with intense pleasure that the boys saw Mr. Harvey suddenly appear on the brow, and checking his horse gaze into the valley.

They leapt to their feet and gave a shout, which was answered by Mr. Harvey.

" Are they round you still? " he shouted.

" No; they have all gone," Dick replied; and Mr. Harvey at once rode down.

By the time he reached them the hunters had freed the legs of the horses, and these struggled to their feet.

" You have given me a nice fright," Mr. Harvey said, as he rode up.

" We have had a pretty good fright ourselves," Dick replied. " If it had not been for Blacking pluckily getting through them to take you the news, I don't think we should have seen daylight. Is he much hurt, sir? "

" He has got a nasty wound," Mr. Harvey replied. " An arrow has gone between his ribs. He fell down from loss of blood when he reached us, and had we gone much farther he would have been overtaken. They were close upon his heels when he got in. Fortunately I halted the caravan soon after you started; when I saw the herds making way I thought it better to wait till you rejoined us. It was well I did so; we noticed him a couple of miles away, and when we saw he was pursued I went out with six men and met him half a mile from the caravan. He had just strength left to tell us what had happened. Then we went back to the caravan, and moved out towards you. We were obliged to come slowly, for there are a good many natives out on the plains, and twice they looked so threatening that I had to laager and treat them to a few distant shots. They evidently did not like the range of my rifle, and so I have come on without any serious fighting. I have been in a great fright about you; but Blacking, when he recovered from his faint, told me that he thought you were safe for a while, as nearly half the party which had been attacking you had followed him, and that you had already killed so many that he thought they would not venture to attack before nightfall. Now, you had better come up to the waggons at once; you can tell me all about it afterwards."

The deer which had formed such useful shelter were now lifted, and in a quarter of an hour the party reached the waggons without molestation. A vigilant watch was kept all night, but no alarm was given.

In the morning Mr. Harvey rode down with the

lads and the hunters into the valley. Except that here and there were deep blood-stains, no signs of the conflict remained, the natives having carried off their dead in the course of the night. The hunters, after examining the ground, declared that fifteen of the enemy had fallen, including those shot on the slopes. The journey was now resumed.

At the next halt the natives came in to trade as usual, and when questioned professed entire ignorance of the attack on the hunters.

Three days later, without further adventure, they arrived at the kraal of the principal chief. It was a large village, and a great number of cattle were grazing in the neighbourhood. The natives had a sullen appearance, but exhibited no active hostility. Mr. Harvey formed his waggons in a laager a few hundred yards outside the village, and then, accompanied by the boys, proceeded to the chief's abode. They were at once conducted to his presence. He was seated in a hut of bee-hive form, rather larger than those which surrounded it. When the white men crawled in through the door, which like all in native structures was not more than three feet high, they were at first unable to see, so dark was the interior. The chief uttered the usual words of welcome.

"I have a complaint to make, chief," Mr. Harvey said, "against some of your people. They attacked my two friends and some of my followers when out hunting. Fortunately they were repulsed, with the loss of some fifteen of their number, but that does not make the attack upon them any the less inexcusable."

" That is bad," the chief said ; " how does my friend, the white trader, know that they were my men ? "

" They were inside your territory anyhow," Mr. Harvey said.   " It was upon the third day after I had left the Matabele."

" It must have been a party of Matabele," the chief said ; " they often come into my territory to steal cattle ; they are bad men—my people are very good."

" I can't prove that they were your people," Mr. Harvey said, " whatever I may think ; but I warn you, chief, that if there is any repetition of the attack while we are in your country you will have no more traders here.   Those who attacked us have learned that we can defend ourselves, and that they are more likely to get death than plunder out of the attempt."

CHAPTER XIV.

TRAPPED IN A DEFILE.

"WHAT do you think of affairs?" Dick asked Mr. Harvey, as, on leaving the chief's hut, they walked back to their waggons.

"For the moment I think we are perfectly safe; the chief would not venture to attack us while we are in his village. In the first place it would put a stop to all trade, and in the second, far as we are from the frontier, he would not feel safe were a massacre to take place in his village. He knows well enough that were a dozen white men to come out to avenge such a deed, with a few waggon-loads of goods to offer to his neighbours as pay for their assistance, he and his tribe would be exterminated. When we are once on our way again we must beware. The feeling among the tribe at the loss they have sustained must be very bitter, although they may repress all outward exhibition of it to us, and if they attack us just as we are on the line between their land and their neighbour's they can deny all knowledge of it. However, they shall not catch us asleep."

"I see the men have put the waggons in laager," Tom said.

"Yes, I told them to do so," Mr. Harvey answered; "it is the custom always with traders travelling north of the Limpopo, and therefore will not be taken as a sign of suspicion of their good faith. A fair index to us of their disposition will be the amount of trade. If they bring their goods freely, we may assume that there is no fixed intention of attacking us; for if they are determined to seize our goods, those who have articles to trade would not care to part with them, when they would hope to obtain a share of our goods for nothing."

The next morning Mr. Harvey spread out a few of his goods, but hardly any of the natives came forward with articles for barter. In the afternoon Mr. Harvey went across to the chief.

"How is it," he asked, "that your people do not bring in their goods for sale? Among the tribes through which I have passed I have done much trade; they see that I give good bargains—your people bring nothing. If they do not wish to trade with the white men, let them say so, and I will tell my brethren that it is of no use to bring their waggons so far."

"My people are very poor," the chief said; "they have been at war with their neighbours, and have had no time to hunt the ostrich or to get skins."

"They cannot have been fighting all the time," Mr. Harvey rejoined; "they must have taken furs and skins—it is clear that they do not wish to trade. To-morrow morning I will go on my way; there are many other tribes who will be glad at the coming of the white trader."

After Mr. Harvey's return to the waggons, it was evident that orders had been issued that some trade should be done, for several parcels of inferior kinds of ostrich feathers and skins were brought in. As it was clear, however, that no genuine trade was to be done, at daybreak the oxen were inspanned, and the caravan continued its journey.

For the next two days the track lay across an open country, and no signs of molestation were met with.

"We are now coming," Mr. Harvey said, "to the very worst part of our journey. The hills we have seen in front of us for the last two days have to be crossed. To-morrow we ascend the lower slopes, which are tolerably easy; but the next day we have to pass through a very wild gorge. The road, which is the bed of a stream, mounts rapidly; but the ravine is nearly ten miles in length. Once at its head we are near the highest point of the shoulder over which we have to cross, and the descent on the other side is comparatively easy. If I could avoid this spot, I would do so; but I know of no other road by which waggons could cross the range for a very long distance either way; this is the one always used by traders. In the wet season it is altogether impassable, for in some places the ravine narrows to fifteen yards, with perpendicular cliffs on either side, and at these points the river, when in flood, rushes down twenty or thirty feet deep. Even putting aside the danger of attack in going through it, I would gladly avoid it if I could, for the weather is breaking ; we have already had some showers, and may get heavy thunderstorms and a tremendous downfall of rain any day.

The next day the journey was an arduous one ; the ground was rough and broken, and the valley up which the road lay was frequently thickly strewn with boulders, which showed the force with which the water in flood-time rushed down over what was now its empty bed.

After a long day's work the caravan halted for the night at the spot where the valley narrowed to the ravine.

"It has been a pretty hard day's work to-day!" Tom said.

"It is nothing to to-morrow's, as you will see," Mr. Harvey replied. "Traders consider this defile to be the very hardest passage anywhere in South Africa, and there are plenty of other bad bits too. In many cases you will see we shall have to unload the waggons, and it will be all that a double team can do to pull them up empty. Sometimes of course the defile is easier than at others ; it depends much upon the action of the last floods. In some years rocks and boulders have been jammed so thickly in the narrow parts that the defile has been absolutely impassable; the following year, perhaps, the obstruction has been swept away, or to a certain extent levelled by the spaces between the rocks being filled up with small stones and sand. How it is this season, I do not know; up to the time we left I had heard of no trader having passed along this way. I have spoken of it as a day's journey, but it is only under the most favourable circumstances that it has ever been accomplished in that time, and sometimes traders have been three or four days in getting through."

Directly the caravan halted Blacking and Jumbo started to examine the defile; it was already growing dusk, and they were only able to get two miles up before it was so dark that they could make their way no further. They returned, saying that the first portion of the defile, which was usually one of the most difficult, was in a bad condition; that many enormous boulders were lying in the bottom; but that it appeared to be practicable, although in some places the waggons would have to be unloaded.

At daybreak the oxen were inspanned, and in a quarter of an hour the leading waggon approached the entrance of the gorge; it seemed cut through a perpendicular cliff, 200 feet high, the gorge through which the river issued appearing a mere narrow crack rent by some convulsion of nature.

"It would be a fearful place to be attacked in," Dick said, " and a few men with rocks up above could destroy us."

"Yes," Mr. Harvey said; "but you see up there?"

Dick looked up, and on one side of the passage saw some tiny figures.

"The three hunters and ten of our men with muskets are up there; they started three hours ago, as they would have to go, Jumbo said, five miles along the face of the cliff before they reached a point where they could make an ascent so as to gain the edge of the ravine. They will keep along parallel with us, and their fire would clear both sides ; it is not usual to take any precaution of this sort, but after our attack of the other day, and the attitude of the chief and his people, we cannot be too cautious. After passing through the first three miles of the defile, the ravine widens into a valley a hundred yards wide ; here they will come down and join us. There are two other ravines, similar to the first, to be passed through, but the country there is so wild and broken that it would be impossible for them to keep along on the heights, and I doubt whether even the natives could find a point from which to attack us."

They had now fairly entered the ravine. For thirty or forty feet up the walls were smooth and polished by the action of the winter torrents ; above, jagged rocks overhung the path, and at some points the cliffs nearly met overhead. Although it was now almost broad daylight, in the depths of this ravine the light was dim and obscure.

The boys at first were awestruck at the scene, but their attention was soon called to the difficulties of the pass. The bed of the stream was covered with rocks of all sizes ; sometimes great boulders, as big as a good-sized cottage, almost entirely blocked the way, and would have done so altogether had not the small boulders round them formed slopes on either side. The depths of the ravine echoed and re-echoed, with a noise like thunder, the shout of the driver and the crack of the whip, as the oxen struggled on. The waggons bumped and lurched along over the stones; the natives and whites all worked their hardest, clearing away the blocks as far as possible from the track required for the waggons. Armed with long wooden levers four or six together prized away the heavy boulders, or, when these were too massive to be moved by their strength, and when no other path could be chosen, piled a number of smaller blocks, so as to make a sort of ascent up which the wheels could travel. The waggons moved but one at a time, the united efforts of the whole party being required to enable them to get along. When the leading waggon had moved forward a hundred yards, the next in succession would be brought up, and so on until the six waggons were again in line; then all hands would set to work ahead, and prepare the path for another hundred yards.

In two places, however, no efforts sufficed to clear the way; the blocks rose in such jagged masses that it was absolutely impossible for the oxen to pull across them,—indeed it was with the greatest difficulty that when unyoked they were one by one got over; then tackles were fastened from the top of the rock to the waggons below—ropes and blocks being generally carried by travellers for such emergencies,—the oxen fastened to the ends of the ropes, and with the purchase so obtained the waggons were dragged bodily one by one over the obstacles.

It was not until late in the afternoon that the party passed safely through the defile and reached the valley beyond, men and animals worn out by the exertions they had undergone.

The day had not passed without excitement, for when they were engaged at the most difficult point of the journey the crack of rifles was heard far overhead, and for half an hour a steady fire was kept up there. Those below were of course wholly ignorant of what was passing there, and for some time they suffered considerable anxiety; for if their guard above had been overpowered they must have been destroyed by rocks cast down by their foes.

At the end of half an hour the firing ceased; but it was not until they camped for the night in the valley beyond the gorge that they learned from the hunters, who joined them there, what had happened. There were, Jumbo explained, three or four hundred natives, but fortunately these approached from the opposite side of the gorge; consequently the little party of defenders was in no danger of attack. The enemy had been disconcerted when they first opened fire, but had then pressed forward to get to the edge of the ravine. The superior weapons of the defenders had, however, checked them, and finding that there was no possibility of coming to close quarters with the little band, they had, after losing several of their number, abandoned the attempt and fallen back.

Soon after nightfall they were startled by a heavy crashing sound, and great rocks came bounding down the sides of the valley. The cattle and waggons were at once moved to the centre of the watercourse, and here they were safe, for the bottom of the valley was so thickly strewn with great boulders that, tremendous as was the force with which the rocks loosened far above came bounding down, these were either arrested or shivered into fragments by the obstacles before they reached the centre of the valley.

No reply to this bombardment of the position was attempted. The enemy were invisible, and there was no clue to their position far up on the hill-side. So long as the rolling down of the rocks was continued, it was certain that no attack at close quarters was intended; consequently, after posting four sentries to arouse them in case of need, the rest of the party, picking out the softest pieces of ground they could find between the stones, lay down to rest.

Before doing so, however, Mr. Harvey had a consultation with the hunters. They said that the next narrow ravine was broken by several lateral defiles of similar character, which came down into it, and that it would therefore be quite impossible to keep along the top; whether there were any points at which the enemy could take post and assail them from above, they knew not.

There was, then, nothing to do but to push steadily on, and early next morning they resumed their way. On the preceding day a slight shower of rain had fallen, but this had been insufficient to increase notably the waters of the streamlet which trickled down among the rocks, for the most part hidden from view. The hunters were of opinion that heavier storms were at hand, and Mr. Harvey agreed with them in the belief.

"We are in a very nasty position, boys," he said, "and I wish now that I had turned south, and made my way down to the Limpopo again, and kept along its banks until past this mountain-range; it would have meant a loss of two months' time, and the country which we shall reach when we get through this defile is a very good one for trade. Still, I am sorry now that I did not adopt that plan; for, what with the natives and the torrent, our position is an extremely serious one; however, there is nothing for it but to push on now. We have passed one out of the three gorges, and even if the other two are in as bad a condition as the one we came up yesterday, two more days' labour will see us through it."

As the caravan moved along the valley the yells of the natives, high up on the slopes, rose loud and menacing. They must have been disgusted at seeing that the labour upon which they had been engaged the whole night, of loosening and setting in motion the rocks, had been entirely thrown away, for they could see that the waggons and teams were wholly uninjured.

As the caravan reached the point where the valley narrowed again, a mile above the halting-place, they began to descend the slopes, as if they meditated an attack, and the rifles of the whites and the three hunters opened fire upon them and checked those on the bare sides of the hill. Many, however, went farther down, and descending into the valley crept up under the shelter of the stones and boulders, and as soon as they came within range opened fire with their bows and arrows. By this time, however, the waggons were entering the ravine which, although at its entrance less abrupt and perpendicular than that below, soon assumed a precisely similar character.

Once well within its shelter Mr. Harvey posted Dick with the three hunters and four of the other natives to defend the rear. This was a matter of little difficulty. Two or three hundred yards up the ravine a barrier, similar to those met with on the previous day, was encountered, and the waggons had to be dragged up by ropes, an operation which took upwards of three hours.

While the passage was being effected, Dick with his party had remained near the mouth of the ravine, and had been busy with the enemy who pressed them; but after the last waggon had safely crossed the barrier they took their station at this point, which they could have held against any number of enemies.

The caravan proceeded on its way, men and animals labouring to the utmost; when, at a point where the sides of rock seemed nearly to close above them, a narrow line of sky only being visible, a great rock came crushing and leaping down, bounding from side to side with a tremendous uproar, and bringing down with it a shower of smaller rocks, which it had dislodged in its course. The bottom of the ravine was here about twelve yards wide, and happened to be unusually level. The great rock, which must have weighed half a ton, fell on one side of the leading waggon and burst into fragments which flew in all directions. Fortunately no one was hurt, but a scream of dismay broke from the natives.

"Steady!" Mr. Harvey shouted; "push on ahead; but each man keep to his work—the first who attempts to run and desert the waggons I will shoot through the head."

"Tom, go on a hundred yards in front, and keep that distance ahead of the leading waggon. Shoot down at once any one who attempts to pass you."

Rock followed rock in quick succession; there was, however, fortunately a bulge in the cliff on the right-hand side, projecting some twenty feet out, and as the blocks struck this they were hurled off to the left side of the path. Seeing this Mr. Harvey kept the waggons close along on the right, and although several of the oxen and three or four of the men were struck by detached fragments from above, or by splinters from the stones as they fell, none were seriously injured.

Long after the caravan had passed the point the rocks continued to thunder down, showing Mr. Harvey that those above were unable to see to the bottom of the gorge, but that they were discharging their missiles at random. A short distance farther a cross ravine, a mere cleft in the rock, some five feet wide at the bottom, was passed, and Mr. Harvey congratulated himself at the certainty that this would bar the progress of their foes above, and prevent the attack being renewed from any point farther on.

At this point so formidable an obstacle was met with in a massive rock, some thirty feet high, jammed in the narrowest part of the ravine, that the waggons had to be emptied and hauled by ropes up the almost perpendicular rock, the oxen being taken through a passage, which with immense labour the men managed to clear of stones, under one of the angles of the rock. It was not until after dark that they reached the spot where the ravine again widened out into a valley, having spent sixteen hours in accomplishing a distance of only three miles. However, all congratulated themselves that two-thirds of their labour was over, and that but one more defile had to be surmounted.

The rear-guard remained encamped at the opening of the defile, but the night passed without interruption, the natives being doubtless disheartened by the failure to destroy the caravan by rocks from above.

"Do you think there is any chance of their attacking us to-night, down the slopes, as they did this morning?" Tom asked Mr. Harvey.

"None whatever," the latter replied, "as you will see in the morning. This valley does not resemble the last; the rocks rise almost perpendicularly on both sides, and it would not be possible for them to make their way down, even if they wanted to do so."

With the first dawn of light the oxen were inspanned. Just as they were starting, one of the natives of Dick's party came up to Mr. Harvey, and reported that the natives in large numbers were showing in the ravine, and the sharp crack of the rifles, which almost at the same moment broke out, confirmed his statement.

"The defile must be held," Mr. Harvey said, "until we are well in the next pass. When the last waggon has entered I will send back word, and they must then follow us and hold the entrance. Tom, you had better take four more of the armed natives to strengthen the rear-guard. Tell Dick to come on and join me. You had your fair share of labour yesterday, and your hands are cut about so, by lifting and heaving rocks, that you would be able to do little to-day. It is rather a good sign that the natives are pressing forward in such force on our rear, as it shows that they have no great faith in any attempt they may make to-day to repeat their rock-throwing experiment of yesterday."

As before two natives were sent on ahead to examine the defile, and Mr. Harvey moved on with the caravan until he reached the upper edge of the valley, which was scarcely half a mile long. Just as he did so the natives came hurriedly down the defile; they reported that a short distance up they had met with another obstacle, to the full as difficult as that which they had got the waggons over on the preceding day, and that, as they turned an angle in the dcfile, and came in sight of it, they were saluted by a shower of arrows, and saw a crowd of natives on the top of the barrier. They had thrown themselves down behind the boulders, and had obtained a good view of the natives and the obstacle. It was some forty feet farther up, and was formed by three or four great boulders jambed in together. On the other side small boulders and stones seemed to have been piled up by the torrent to the level of the rocks; but on the lower side it was almost perpendicular, and they questioned if a man could climb it,—certainly there was no passage for oxen.

CHAPTER XV.

A MOUNTAIN-TORRENT.

THE news brought by the scouts was very serious. The continued·fire in the rear showed that the enemy were making a serious attack in that quarter. But Mr. Harvey feared that his fighting force there must be weakened greatly, to enable him to attack so formidable a position as that which the enemy occupied in front. Before arriving at any decision as to his best course, he halted the caravan, and went forward himself, with the two natives, to inspect the position which they had discovered.

When he reached the turn in the defile he crawled forward among the boulders until he reached a spot where he could obtain a clear view of the barrier; it was to the full as formidable as it had been described by the scouts It would have needed an active man to scale the rocks without any opposition from above, while on the top a dense body of natives were clustered, numbering at least fifty, and probably a considerable portion of their force was concealed from view.

Mr. Harvey sent back one of the natives to tell Dick to come on and join him; after which he was to go back and bid Jumbo come up, as Mr. Harvey had great confidence in the hunter's shrewdness.

Dick presently arrived, and was much impressed with the formidable nature of the obstacle.

"We might creep forward," he said, "among the stones and soon drive those fellows off the edge, but they would only lie down behind, and could easily destroy us, as we climbed one by one to the top. Each one, as he got up, would be riddled with assegais. What are you thinking of doing, sir?"

"I don't know what is best, Dick. I quite agree with you, it is a tremendous position to storm, but on the other hand it would be almost as bad to retreat."

Ten minutes later Jumbo arrived at a run; without a word he threw himself down by the side of Mr. Harvey, and for two or three minutes gazed silently at the obstacle ahead; then, to Mr. Harvey's surprise, he turned over on to his back, and lay there with his eyes open.

"What on earth are you doing, Jumbo?"

"Look there, sir," the native said, pointing to a glistening spot, the size of a crown-piece, on his stomach.

"Well, what of that?" Mr. Harvey said; "that's a drop of rain—there's another fallen on my hat. What do you think of that place ahead?"

"Me no think nothing about him, sir; that place, sir, no consequence one way or de other. You hear him, sir?"

As he spoke a louder crash of thunder burst overhead. Mr. Harvey looked up now. That portion of the sky which could be seen was inky black. Great drops of rain were falling with a pattering sound on the rock.

"Storm come, sir; very bad storm. I see him coming, and say to Massa Tom, 'Two or tree hour fight over; now you see someting like a mountain-storm. In tree hours water come down twenty feet deep.'"

"You are right, Jumbo. It is lucky the storm has begun so early; if we had got far into the defile we should have been caught. Now, all we have got to do is to wait. Go back, Dick, and send up every man with fire-arms; we must at once engage those fellows in front and occupy their attention. If they once perceive their danger they will make a desperate rush down here, and it will go hard with us then. When you have sent the fighting-men up, see that the teamsters move all the waggons to the highest piece of ground you can find in the valley. Let them arrange the waggons there as closely as they will pack, and keep the animals well round them. A flood will destroy our enemy, but I am not sure that it may not destroy us too. Now hurry away, and tell the fighting-men to run up as quick as they can. When you have seen everything in readiness, join Tom, and warn him to be ready to fall back to the waggons as soon as the flood comes."

Dick ran down the ravine. It was not until he issued from it that he was aware how tremendously the rain was pouring down. In the defile he had been

conscious only of a slight mist, with an occasional drop
of heavy rain, for very few of the rain-drops which
entered the gap far above descended to the bottom,
almost all striking against the sides. In the comparatively open valley, however, the rain was coming down
in a perfect cataract. Dick at once sent all the
fighting-men to the front, and three minutes later the
report of musketry told that they were engaged with
the enemy.

Dick now set to work with ten of the natives to
select the spot on which to place the waggons. The
bottom of the valley was very flat, and the sand
between the boulders showed that when the water was
high the whole was covered. He, however, found a
spot on the left-hand side, about midway between the
two defiles, which was some feet higher than the rest.
The hill-side behind at this point rose somewhat less
abruptly than elsewhere, and it was probable that the
rise in the bottom was formed by a slip which had
taken place at some past period. Here the waggons
were arranged side by side in two rows, the wheels
of the three inner waggons close against the slope
above them. The cattle were gathered closely
round.

Dick then joined Tom, whom he found in high
spirits, the hunters having already told him that the
flood would very soon come to their relief. The
party was hotly engaged. About thirty or forty
yards intervened between them and their enemy,
who, crouching behind rocks, were shooting their

arrows high into the air, so that they came down almost perpendicularly upon the defenders. One of these had been killed and three severely wounded by the missiles; while they themselves could only get an occasional shot at a limb exposed beyond the shelter of the boulders.

Not having received orders to stay by Tom, Dick retraced his steps up the valley to the party above. From the cliffs at the side of the valley waterfalls were leaping down, and a stream of water was already beginning to flow down its centre. The bed of the defile was perfectly dry, the stones being scarcely wetted by the fine mist from above. Dick found Mr. Harvey and the natives engaged in keeping up a hot fire at the top of the obstacle, lying at a distance of forty or fifty yards from it among the rocks. One or two dead natives were stretched on the top of the rock; the rest were not to be seen, but the arrows whistled fast over his head, showing that they were lying down just behind it.

"The rain is tremendous outside," Dick said, as he joined Mr. Harvey. "You can have no idea what it is here. The water is pouring so fast into the valley that a stream is forming there already, and will soon be running two or three feet deep down the lower pass. I wonder it has not begun to make its way down from above."

"It has begun, Dick; look at those little threads of water between the stones. When it comes, it will come with a rush; that is always the way with these gorges. Jumbo is listening ; it will come with a roar like thunder. He has just told me I had better send most of the men back at once, keeping only four or five to continue firing to the last moment. You see the enemy, who are there on a sort of platform, will not notice the water that is making its way down. See how fast it rises ; it is ankle-deep already—and, I tell you, we shall have to run when the time comes."

All the natives, with the exception of Jumbo and two other men, were sent back.

" I don't see anything to fire at," Dick said.

" No," Mr. Harvey agreed ; " it is a pure waste of ammunition, except that it occupies their attention. They can hardly be conscious yet how tremendously it is raining. If they were they would not remain where they are, but would make a rush upon us, however great the risk."

" Listen ! " Jumbo exclaimed suddenly.

They listened and were conscious of a dull, heavy, roaring sound. Jumbo leapt to his feet.

" Come ! " he said ; " run for your lives."

They started up and took to their heels. A terrible yell was heard behind them, and, glancing over his shoulder, as he turned the corner, Dick saw the natives climbing down from their defence, and even leaping from the top in their terror. Fast as Dick was running, the roar behind rose louder and louder.

" Quick, Dick," Mr. Harvey shouted, " or you will be too late."

Dick hurried to the utmost, but the stream was already rising rapidly, and was running knee-deep between the stones. Stumbling and slipping, and cutting himself against the rocks, Dick struggled on. The mighty roar was now close behind him, and seemed to him like that of a heavy train at full speed. He reached the mouth of the ravine; the water was already up to his waist. Mr. Harvey and Jumbo dashed in, seized him by the arms, and dragged him out.

"Run!" they said.

They were not fifty yards from the mouth, when Dick, looking round, saw a mighty wall of water, fifteen feet high, leap from it, pouring as from huge sluice-gates into the valley. He did not stop running until he joined the rest gathered by the waggons.

Tom and his party were already there, for the rising water had soon warned their assailants of the danger, and the fire had suddenly ceased. Already the greater part of the valley was covered with water, down the centre of which a foaming torrent was flowing. Here and there could be seen numerous dark objects, which, he knew, were the bodies of the enemy who had defended the upper defile, caught before they could reach its mouth by the wall of water from above. They had instantly been dashed lifeless against the rocks and boulders, and not one could be seen to make towards the comparatively still waters on either side of the centre stream.

Driven back again by the narrow entrance to the

lower defile the water in the valley rose rapidly, as with an ever-increasing violence it poured in from above. There it was rushing out in a solid, dark-brown cataract, which Dick judged to be fully forty feet in height. In a quarter of an hour from its first outburst the water had already reached the feet of those standing upon the little knoll of ground in the valley. The oxen lowing and stamping with terror pressed more and more closely together. The young ostriches were placed in one of the waggons, for although their height would have left their heads well above water, they would probably have succumbed to the effects of a prolonged submersion of their bodies.

" If it goes on like this for another quarter of an hour," Mr. Harvey said, " the oxen will be washed away, if not the waggons. Thank God, I think we can all manage to climb up the slope. Jumbo, tell the men each to load themselves with five or six days' provisions. Let half a dozen take boxes of ammunition, and as many bales of the best cloth. Let the rest take as many bundles of the best ostrich feathers as they can carry. Let them lay them all on the slope, twenty or thirty yards up, wherever they can find place for them, and then come down again, and make as many trips with the best goods as they can."

All hands worked hard; inch by inch the water rose; Mr. Harvey, assisted by the boys and teamsters, fastened ropes together, and with these surrounded the closely-packed throng of cattle. The water was now more than waist-deep, and was still rising;

soon the cattle on the outside were lifted off their feet. There was no current here, and they floated with their heads on the backs of those in front of them; higher and higher the water rose, till the whole of the cattle were afloat. At first a few struggled, but soon they subsided into quiet, and the whole mass floated together, with only their heads above water.

On every available ledge on the hillside were placed bundles and bales of all kinds, and here the whites and natives stood, watching the progress of the flood. The thunder-shower had ceased soon after the water first burst through the gorge, but Mr. Harvey knew that some hours must elapse before the flood would begin to abate.

"I don't see why the water should not run off as fast as it comes in," Dick said.

"It all depends, Dick, upon the question whether in the lower defile there is any place narrower than the mouth, through which the water is rushing from above. According to appearances this is so; for, could the water escape faster than it comes in, the lake here would cease to rise. I think now the water has reached a level, where the outflow nearly equals the inflow. I have been watching the wheels of the waggons, and for the last ten minutes I do not think it has risen above an inch or two."

"I will get down and watch," Dick said, and he scrambled down to the water's edge.

Two minutes later he shouted up,—

"It has not risen at all since I came here!"

The teamsters had taken their station on the outside waggons, and continued to talk and shout to the oxen, exhorting these to be patient and quiet, as if the animals were capable of understanding every word they said.

For three hours there was no change in the situation. Then all thought that there was a slight decrease in the height of the torrent of water pouring from the defile, and half an hour later a slight but distinct subsidence in the level of the water could be perceived. In another hour it had fallen a foot, and after that the fall was rapid and steady. The deep roar caused by the rushing torrent and the rumbling of the huge boulders and rocks swept along in the narrow defile, gradually subsided, and soon the bullocks were again standing on their feet.

The natives set to work to wash away the thick sediment which the flood had left on the floor of the waggons, and before nightfall the goods were all repacked. But few signs of the recent flood now remained in the valley. A stream still rushed through the centre. Trunks and branches of trees lay here and there, as the water had left them, and the bodies of some twenty or thirty natives were lying amongst the rocks. In some places shallow pools remained; in others were sheets of glistening mud.

"We shall have no more trouble with the natives,' Mr. Harvey said; "the fighting-men of that tribe must have been nearly annihilated."

"Do you think that those below were caught, as well as those above?"

"Certainly," Mr. Harvey answered; "the water went down with the speed of a race-horse; they had only a few minutes' start, and would have been over-taken before they could have even gained the lower bed of the gorge. We can journey on peacefully now. We have been fortunate indeed; we have only lost one man, and the three who were hit with stones are all likely to do well. We have not lost a single bullock, nor a bale of goods."

"We shall have hard work to get the waggons up that place where the natives made the stand to-morrow."

"It is quite likely," Mr. Harvey said, "that the obstacle there no longer exists. A flood like that of to-day would carry away anything. Look at those great blocks, some of which must weigh more than a hundred tons. Likely enough some of them have formed part of that great pile. I have already sent Tony and Blacking up the defile to see how the flood has left it, and in an hour they will be back to report."

The hunters on returning brought the good news that the great block had been removed, and so far as they had explored no other of any importance had been found. They said indeed that the defile was now more open than either of the two gorges they had already passed through.

This was very satisfactory, for all had had enough of lifting and heaving rocks. Their hands were all cut and wounded, and every limb ached with the strains which they had undergone.

The next morning at daybreak the caravan started. The hunters' report of the state of the roads was fairly borne out, and although some difficulties were met with it was unnecessary to unyoke the oxen, although of course many boulders had to be cleared away to allow them to pass. On emerging at the upper end of the defile they found they were in a valley which opened out to a great width, and rose in gradual slopes at its head to the crest of the hills. As the only egress at the lower end was by the defile, it was clear that the whole rainfall must make its way by this exit, which fully accounted for the tremendous torrent they had witnessed.

Two days' travelling brought them to the foot of the slopes on the other side of the range of hills, and they were soon engaged in carrying on a considerable trade with the natives there.

For another three months they travelled slowly through the country, by the end of which time they had disposed of all their goods, and the waggons were filled to the tilts with skins and bales of ostrich feathers.

They now turned their faces to the south. After journeying for a fortnight they perceived one day, far across the country, the white tilts of another caravan. The three whites at once started at full gallop, eager to hear news of what had taken place in the colony during their absence. As they neared the caravan two white men rode out to meet them;

both were known to Mr. Harvey, and hearty greetings were exchanged.

The new-comers were halting for the day, and Mr. Harvey and the boys were soon seated in tents, with three bottles of beer in front of them, a luxury which they heartily enjoyed, having been many months without tasting it.

"And now what is the news in the colony?" Mr. Harvey asked, after having replied to their questions as to the state of trade, and the route which they had followed, as the new-comers would of course take another line, so as not to pass over the same ground.

"Things don't look well," they answered; "the Boers are growing so insolent that there is no getting on with them. Several English have been shot down in various places, without the smallest cause. They openly declare their intention of recovering their independence. The English stores are for the most part tabooed, and things altogether look very threatening. There is a mere handful of British troops in the Transvaal, and only a regiment or so in Natal. Those wretched duffers at home hurried every soldier out of the country the instant the fighting was over, and if the Boers really mean business we shall have no end of trouble. You see, we have crushed their two enemies, the Zulus and Secoceni, and now that we have done the work for them they want to get rid of us."

"I thought we should have trouble with them," Mr. Harvey said; "they are an obstinate, pig-headed race; they never would pay taxes to their own government; they would not even turn out and fight when Secoceni threatened to overrun the country; and now, as likely as not, they will fight desperately for the independence they were glad enough to relinquish in the hour of danger. What you tell me is a nuisance. I had originally intended to go down through Kimberley to Port Elizabeth; but I changed my mind and decided to go back again through the Transvaal, and I have come so far to the east that I do not like to change my plans again. However, I don't suppose we shall be interfered with. They can't very well quarrel with us, if we won't quarrel with them."

"Perhaps not," the trader said; "but I tell you I have found it precious difficult to keep my temper several times. The insolence and swagger of those fellows is amazing."

The two caravans halted near each other for the day, and a pleasant evening was spent. The next morning each resumed its way.

No further adventure was met with until the Limpopo was reached; this was crossed on rafts. The natives who had accompanied them were now paid off, receiving a handsome present each, in addition to the sum agreed upon, and the caravan proceeded on its way.

At the first Dutch village at which they arrived, a week after leaving the Limpopo, they had evidence of a change of demeanour in the Boers. As they passed through the streets a group of five or six men were standing at the door of a store ; one of them in a loud and insolent voice made a remark to the others, that before long they would not have any of these English dogs going through their country—a remark which was received with boisterous approval by the others. Mr. Harvey's face flushed, and he was on the point of reining in his horse, and riding up to chastise the insolent Boer, but the thought of the distance of country yet before him checked him.   It was clearly the intention of the man to force a quarrel, and in this the English were sure to get the disadvantage finally. He therefore rode quietly on with the insolent laughter of the Dutchmen ringing in his ears. The lads were equally indignant, and it was only the example of Mr. Harvey which had restrained them.

"Things have come to a pretty pass," Mr. Harvey said, as he dismounted, "that Englishmen should be openly insulted in this way. However, I suppose it will not do to resent it, for these scoundrels would clearly be only too glad of an excuse to shoot us down; but if this sort of thing is going on at every village we pass through, we shall have hard work in keeping our tempers until we are fairly out of the Transvaal. I pity our countrymen who have bought land or set up stores in this country. I was never fond of the Boers, though I am willing to allow that they are a splendid set of men, and that they are magnificent riders and good shots. I question if we shall ever retain them against their will. Of course if we had a government which worked with energy and decision it would be a different matter altogether. There are a considerable number of English and Scotch settlers already here, and the natives would rise against the Dutch to a man, if called upon to do so; and if a couple of dozen of their ringleaders were promptly seized and shot, there would be an end to the whole matter. But I know what it will be: the natives will not be encouraged or even allowed to rise, our soldiers, who can hardly hit a haystack at a hundred yards, will be shot down at a distance by the Boers, and, likely enough, we shall meet with a serious disaster, and then the English government will get frightened and make any terms these fellows demand.

CHAPTER XVI.

A FIGHT WITH THE BOERS.

FOR some time they continued their journey, meeting everywhere with the grossest incivility on the part of the Boers; in many places they were refused water at the farms, and warned at once off the land, and Mr. Harvey had the greatest difficulty in keeping his own temper and restraining the boys from resenting the language of the Boers.

One day, as they were riding along, two Boers on horseback halted on an eminence near the road and addressed taunting remarks to them; they made no answer, but continued their way. They had not gone a hundred yards when one of the Boers deliberately took aim and fired at them; the ball passed between Dick and Mr. Harvey and struck one of the natives walking just in front of them, killing him upon the spot. This was too much. Mr. Harvey and the lads wheeled their horses, unslung their rifles, and fired at the Boers, who were galloping away. One of them at once dropped from his saddle, shot through the head; the other reeled, but, retaining his seat, galloped off at full speed.

"This is a bad business, boys," Mr. Harvey said; "we could not help it, but it will bring trouble upon us. Now let us branch off from the road we are following, and make for Leydenberg ; we are within three days' march of that place. There is an English garrison there, and justice will be done. If we push on straight for Standerton, we shall be overtaken and probably killed before we get there."

The bullocks' heads were turned towards the south-east, and at the best pace the teams were driven across the country. Several large native kraals were passed in the course of the day, and after a march of nearly double the ordinary length the caravan halted for the night on the banks of a stream. A sharp watch was kept all night, but nothing particular happened.

Just as they were about to inspan the oxen in the morning some fifteen or twenty men were seen approaching at a gallop. The oxen were at once driven again to the laager, and every man seized his arms. The Dutchmen halted at a distance of a hundred yards, and then three of them rode up to the caravan.

"What do you want ?" Mr. Harvey said, advancing on foot in front of the waggons, while the lads and the three hunters stood, rifles in hand, behind them.

"We summon you to surrender," the Boers said ; "you have murdered Mr. Van Burer and wounded Mr. Schlessihoff."

"We have done nothing of the sort," Mr. Harvey answered. "We were going quietly along the road when those men insulted us ; we passed on without answering. After we had gone a hundred yards they fired at us, narrowly missed me, and killed one of my men. We fired back, and with the result you have named. We are quite ready to answer for our conduct, and when we get to Leydenberg we shall at once deliver ourselves up to the magistrate, and report what has occurred, and you can then bring any charge you want to make against us."

"You will never get to Leydenberg," the Boers said scoffingly; "we are your magistrates and judges; we want no English law here. Once for all, will you surrender?"

"We certainly will not," Mr. Harvey replied, "and if you molest us it will be at your peril."

Without another word the Boers turned their horses' heads and rode back to their comrades; upon their joining them the whole rode some little distance to the rear, and then divided, half turning to the left, the other to the right.

"What on earth are they going to do?" Dick asked in surprise.

"They are going to surround us," Mr. Harvey said; "they will dismount and leave their horses in shelter. Now, lads, out with all the bales of skins and pile them up under the waggons."

All hands set to work, and soon under each waggon a thick breastwork of bales was erected, reaching nearly up to the floor, leaving only enough space to see out of and fire; the three whites and the hunters took station, one under each waggon, the teamsters and other natives being distributed round the square. Quickly as they had laboured, the preparations were not complete, when from a brow, at the distance of about a hundred yards from the laager, a shot was fired, the bullet burying itself with a thud in one of the bales of skins; almost instantly from every point in a circle round other shots were fired, and the splintering of wood and the dull sounds, as the shots struck the barricade, told how accurate was their aim.

Mr. Harvey's orders had been, " Don't throw away a shot. When you see the flash of a rifle, aim steadily at that point ; the next time a head is lifted to take aim, hit it." The natives were ordered on no account to fire, unless the Boers attempted to close, but to lie quietly under shelter of the defences. In consequence of these orders not a shot replied to the first volley of the Boers ; but when the second round commenced, puffs of smoke darted from beneath the waggons. Dick and Tom knew that their shots had been successful, for the heads at which they had aimed lay clearly in view, and no discharge came from the rifles pointed towards them. The other shots must have passed near their marks, and after this first exhibition of the shooting powers of the defenders, the Boers became much more careful, firing only at intervals, and shifting their ground each time, before they raised their heads to take aim. So the whole day passed, a dropping fire being kept up on both sides. The defenders were convinced by the end of the day that seven or eight of the Boers had fallen, but their places had been more than filled by new-comers who had been seen galloping across the plain towards the scene of conflict. On the side of the defenders no casualties had occurred.

Towards evening the fire died away, and Tom and Dick joined Mr. Harvey.

"What will they do next?"

"I don't know, Dick; the Boers are by no means fond of exposing themselves to danger, as has been proved over and over again in their fights with natives. They must have suffered already a great deal more than they bargained for, and are no doubt heartily sick of the job. They may try a rush at night, though I question whether they will do so. I rather imagine that their tactics will be to besiege us until we are driven to make a move, and then to attack us by the way. Fortunately the stream is close at hand, and we can get water for our cattle. Still, there must be an end of it at some time or other."

Blacking now crept under the waggon.

"Massa, what you say?—me think the best plan will be for me to crawl out and run to chief Mangrope; his place twenty miles away; he always hate the Dutch, and refuse to pay tribute; several times they have sent parties against him, but he always beat them off. Blacking tell him that de Boers attack English, and that if he come down and help drive them off you give him one team of fine oxen,—he come."

"I think your plan is a very good one, Blacking; but do you think that you can get through?"

"Get through those stupid Boers? Easily," Blacking said contemptuously.

"Very well, Blacking; then, as soon as it is dark, you had better start."

Blacking nodded and withdrew, and an hour afterwards stole out from the camp.

As soon as night fell the Boers opened fire again, this time aiming entirely at the end of the waggons nearest the water, evidently with the intention of rendering it difficult to procure water from the stream.

Mr. Harvey and his companions answered by firing at the flashes. As they hoped that rescue would arrive ere long, Mr. Harvey did not permit any one to go outside shelter to fetch water, as the animals had been watered in the morning the first thing, and could, if necessary, hold out until the following night.

Just as daylight was breaking a tremendous yell was heard, followed by a hasty discharge of muskets; then there was the sound of horses' hoofs galloping at full speed, and then, headed by Blacking, two to three hundred natives came up to the camp. The chief himself was among them. Mr. Harvey had on several occasions traded with him, and now thanked him warmly for the welcome aid he had brought him.

The Boers were already far away, each man having run to his horse and galloped off, panic-stricken at the sudden attack. The oxen were at once inspanned, two being taken from each team and presented to the chief, together with a large bale of cotton in return for his assistance. The caravan then started, and after a march of sixteen hours arrived at Leydenberg.

"It is an awful nuisance," Dick said to Tom on the march, "our being obliged to come round here.

If everything had gone straight, I calculated that we might be at home by Christmas-eve. Now, goodness only knows when we shall arrive; for, as likely as not, we may be kept here for days over this row with the Boers."

The moment they arrived at Leydenberg Mr. Harvey, accompanied by the two lads and the three native hunters, went to the house of the magistrate. That gentleman had just finished his dinner; but on being told that his visitors' business was urgent he asked them to be shown in. The hunters remained outside, and the lads followed Mr. Harvey into the house.

"I have come to make a complaint against some Boers," the trader said.

"Then I can tell you beforehand," the magistrate put in, "that your mission is a vain one. Outside this town I have not at present the slightest authority. Complaints reach me on all sides of outrages perpetrated by the Boers upon English settlers and traders. Strong armed parties are moving about the country; and although I will of course hear anything that you have got to say, with a view of obtaining redress when things settle down again, I cannot hold out any hope of being able to take action at present."

"I have scarcely come to you, sir, with the idea of obtaining redress, but rather of stating my case, in case the Boers should bring a complaint against me."

The trader then proceeded to relate the circumstances which had occurred: the wanton attack upon them in the first place, the murder of one of their servants, the killing of one and the wounding of the other of the aggressors, the subsequent attack upon their camp, and their relief by Mangrope.

"I think you have got remarkably well out of the affair, and although the attack of the Boers has cost you the life of one of your followers and twelve oxen, as you have killed eight or ten of them you have made matters more than even, and have, moreover, given them a lesson which may be useful. I will take down your depositions, as it is as well that your friends here, and the hunters you speak of, should testify to it. It is hardly likely that I shall hear any more of the matter; the Boers were clearly in the wrong, and in any case they would not be likely at the present moment, when the country is in a state very closely approaching insurrection, to seek redress in an English court. Fortunately 250 men of the 94th Regiment leave here to-morrow morning, on the way to Pretoria. Their road will, for some distance, be the same as yours; their colonel is at the present moment in the next room with several of his officers, and I will request permission for your waggons to follow his baggage-train. Thus you can keep with him until the road separates, by which time you will be well out of the district of the Boers who attacked you. You will, I suppose, go through Utrecht and keep the eastern road, as that will be shorter than going round by Standerton and Newcastle. If you will wait here for a few minutes, I will speak to the colonel."

In a short time the magistrate returned, saying that Mr. Harvey's six waggons might join the baggage-train of the 94th on the following morning.

At eight o'clock the 94th marched from Leydenberg, and Mr. Harvey's waggons fell in the rear of the column. As they had a considerable amount of baggage and stores, the column would not proceed at a faster rate than the ordinary pace of the bullock-train.

When the column was once on the march, the colonel rode down the line and entered into conversation with Mr. Harvey and the lads, who were riding with him, and after having heard the narrative of the fight with the Boers, he said to the lads, "You have had a baptism of fire early."

Mr. Harvey smiled.

"They have had some very much more serious fighting in the country north of the Limpopo ; besides, they were both present at Isandula, Kambula, and Ulundi."

"Indeed !" the colonel said ; "then they have seen fighting. Perhaps you will ride on with me to the head of the column again ; we have a long day's march before us, and if your young friends will give us some of their experiences it will while away the time."

The four cantered together to the head of the column, where the doctor and one or two other officers were riding. After a word or two of introduction the colonel asked the lads to tell them how they came to be at Isandula, and how they escaped to tell the tale.

"You had better tell it, Dick," Tom said; "you are a better hand at talking than I."

Dick accordingly proceeded to relate their adventures during the Zulu war, and the story excited great interest among the officers. When the column halted for the day, the colonel invited Mr. Harvey and the lads to dine at the mess, and would not listen to any excuse on the ground that their clothes were better suited for travelling among the native tribes than for dining at a regimental mess.

The dinner was a very pleasant one, and after the cloth had been removed and cigars were lit, Mr. Harvey, at the colonel's request, related their adventures north of the Limpopo.

"Your life is indeed an adventurous one," he said, when the trader had finished. "It needs endurance, pluck, coolness, and a steady finger on the trigger. You may truly be said, indeed, to carry your lives in your hands."

"Our present journey has been an exceptionally adventurous one," Mr. Harvey said, "and you must not suppose that we are often in the habit of fighting our way. I have indeed on several occasions been in very perilous positions, and some other evening, before we separate, I shall be glad, if it will interest you, to relate one or two of them."

"By the way," the colonel said, when they took their

leave, "remember, the word for the night is, 'Newcastle.' You will probably be challenged several times by sentries before you get to your waggons, for, although there is no absolute insurrection at present, there is no saying when the Boers may break out. They will hardly think of attacking a body of troops marching peaceably along ; still, it is as well to neglect no precautions. If you are challenged, 'Who comes there?' you will reply, 'Friends.' The sentry will then say, 'Advance and give the word.' You walk forward and say, 'Newcastle,' and you will pass all right."

The march was continued for four days. At the end of this time they arrived at the spot where the direct road for Pieter-Maritzburg through Utrecht left that which they were following.

"Look here, lads," Mr. Harvey said ; "this road will take you considerably out of your way. If you like you can follow the column for another couple of days. You will then cross the south road, and can there leave them and gallop on by yourselves to Standerton in one day, and home the next. That will take you back by the 23rd ; whereas, if you go on with me, you will not be back by New Year's Day. We are getting now to a part of the colony where the English element is pretty strong, and the Boers are not likely to be troublesome ; so I shall have no difficulty in passing down with the waggons. You can tell your fathers that we have had a most satisfactory trip, and I expect when I have sold our goods at Durban they will have good reason to be content."

The lads gladly accepted the offer; they were longing to be at home again, and especially wished to be back by Christmas.

The colonel on hearing of the arrangement heartily invited the lads to mess with the regiment for the time that they continued with them, and offered to have a spare tent pitched for their accommodation.

CHAPTER XVII.

A TERRIBLE JOURNEY.

THAT evening Mr. Harvey and the lads were again invited to dine at mess, and after dinner the colonel asked Mr. Harvey if he would be good enough to tell them some of his adventures in the interior.

"I have had so many," the trader said, "that I hardly know which would be most interesting. I have been many times attacked by the natives, but I do not know that any of these affairs were so interesting as the fight we had in the defile the other day. Some of the worst adventures which we have to go through are those occasioned by want of water. I have had several of these, but the worst was one which befell me on one of my earliest trips up the country. On this occasion I did not as usual accompany my father, but went with a trader named MacGregor, a Scotchman, as my father was ill at the time. He considered me too young to go by myself, and when he proposed to MacGregor that I should join him with the usual number of waggons he sent up, MacGregor objected, saying,—I have no doubt with justice,—that the double amount of goods would be more than could be disposed of. He added, however, that he should be glad if I would accompany him with a couple of waggons. It was, as it turned out, a very good thing for my father that his venture was such a small one. MacGregor was a keen trader; he understood the native character well, and was generally very successful in his ventures. His failing was that he was an obstinate, pig-headed man, very positive in his own opinions, and distrusting all advice given him.

"Our trip had been a successful one. We penetrated very far in the interior, and disposed of all our goods. When we had done so, we started to strike down to Kimberley across a little-known and very sandy district. The natives among whom we were, endeavoured to dissuade MacGregor from making the attempt, saying that the season was a very dry one, that many of the pools were empty, and that there would be the greatest difficulty in obtaining water. MacGregor disregarded the advice. By taking the direct route south he would save some hundreds of miles. He said that other caravans had at different times taken this route in safety, and at the same time of the year. He insisted that the season had not been a particularly dry one, and that he was not going to be frightened by old women's tales. The natives were always croaking about something, but he did not mean to lose a month of his time for nothing.

"Accordingly we started. The really bad part of our journey was about 150 miles across a sandy country, with low scrub. The bullocks, when driven to it, would eat the leaves of this scrub, so that we did not anticipate any difficulty in the way of forage. In the wet season many streams run across the country and find their way into the Limpopo. In summer they dry up, and water is only obtained in pools along their courses. There were twelve waggons in the caravan—ten belonging to MacGregor, and my two. I had with me a servant, a native, who had been for years in the employment of my father, a very faithful and trustworthy fellow.

"At the end of the first day's march of fifteen miles we found water at the spot to which our native guide led us. The second day the pool was found to be dry. We got there early, having started before daybreak, for the heat was tremendous. On finding the pool empty I rode ten miles down the course of the stream, and MacGregor as far up it, but found no water, and on getting back to the camp the oxen were inspanned, and we made another march; here we found water, and halted next day.

"So we went on, until we were half-way across the desert. Several of the marches had been double ones, the track was heavy from the deep sand, some of the oxen had died, and all were much reduced in strength. Although MacGregor was not a man to allow that he had been wrong, I saw that he was anxious, and before advancing he sent on a horseman and the native guide two days' journey to see how the water held out. On their return they reported that twenty miles in front there was a pool of good water, and that thirty miles farther there was a small supply, which was, however, rapidly drying up. MacGregor determined to push on. The first day's march was got through, although five or six more oxen dropped by the way. The second was a terrible march; I have never known a hotter day in South Africa, and one felt blinded and crushed by the heat. The weakened teams could scarcely draw the waggons along, and by nightfall but half the journey had been performed. The oxen were turned loose and allowed for an hour or two to crop the bush; then they were inspanned again. All night long we continued our march; when, just at sunrise, we got to the place where water had been found, the pool was empty—the two days' sun since the horseman had been there had completely dried it up. We set to work to dig a hole; but the sand was shallow, the rock lying but a foot or two below, and we only got a few buckets of water, but just enough to give a swallow to each of the oxen and horses. Again we searched far up and down the course of the stream, but without success; we dug innumerable holes in its bed, but without finding water.

"We were still fifty miles from safety; but in that fifty miles the natives said that they did not think a drop of water would be found, as this was notoriously the driest point on the route. Half the oxen had now died, and MacGregor determined to leave all but two of the waggons behind, to harness teams of the strongest of those remaining, and to drive the rest alongside. We halted till night to allow the animals to feed, and then started. We got on fairly enough until daybreak; then the sun rose, and poured down upon us. It was a terrible day. No one spoke, and the creaking of the wheels of the waggons was the only sound to be heard. Every mile we went the numbers lessened, as the bullocks lay down to die by the way. My tongue seemed to cleave to the roof of my mouth, and the sun to scorch up my brain. I hardly took notice of what was going on around me, but let the reins hang loose on my horse's neck. Several times he stumbled, and at last fell heavily. I picked myself up from the sands, and saw that he was dying. The waggons had come to a standstill now, and I had, I saw, for the last quarter of a mile gone on alone. I looked at my watch; it was four o'clock, and I turned and walked slowly back to the waggons. The drivers had unroped the oxen, but most of them lay where they had halted, incapable of rising to their feet; others had tottered to the shade cast by the waggons, and had thrown themselves down there. The drivers were lying among them. As I came up MacGregor staggered towards me; he was chewing a handful of leaves. 'I have been wrong, Harvey,' he said, in a hoarse voice, 'and it has cost us all our lives. Say you forgive me, my boy.' 'I forgive you heartily,' I said; 'you thought it was for the best.' I don't remember much more. I lay down and wondered vaguely what had become of my man, whom I had not seen since we started on the previous evening.

"The next thing I remember was that it was night.

I got up on my feet and staggered to a bullock that I heard faintly groaning; I cut a vein in his neck and sucked the blood, and then started to walk; fortunately, as it turned out, I had not gone a hundred yards when a dizziness came over me, and I fell again to the ground. I must have lain there for some hours; when I became conscious, water was being poured between my lips. I soon recovered sufficiently to sit up, and found that it was my faithful man. When the caravan started from the last halting-place, he had seen that it was impossible for it to reach its journey's end, and although, like the rest, he was exhausted and worn out, he had started at full speed alone, and by morning reached water, having travelled fifty miles in the night. It was midday before he succeeded in finding a native kraal; then by promise of a large reward he induced forty men, each laden with a heavy skin of water, to start with him, and at three in the morning reached the camp; fortunately he stumbled across me just before he got there.

" The assistance arrived in time. Two of the drivers were found to be dead, but MacGregor and the other hands, sixteen in number, were all brought round. The supply carried by the natives was sufficient to give an ample drink to the eighteen oxen which were still alive. A feed of maize was then given to each, but as they were too weak to drag even one of the waggons they were driven on ahead, and most of them got over the twenty-five miles which still separated them from water. We halted there a week, to allow the animals to recover; then, carrying skins of water for their supply on the way, they went back and brought in the two waggons, one at a time. With these I came down to the colony. MacGregor remained behind, and directly the rain set in went up with native cattle and brought down the other waggons, all the valuable contents of which, however, had in the intervening time been carried off by natives. It was a near squeak, wasn't it? MacGregor was never the same man again, and shortly after his return to Natal he sold off his waggons and went back to Scotland. Being young and strong I soon recovered from my privation."

"Lions are very abundant in some parts of the interior, are they not, Mr. Harvey?" one of the officers asked, after they had thanked the trader for his story.

"Extraordinarily so," Mr. Harvey replied; "in fact it has long been a puzzle among us how such vast quantities could find food—in no other country in the world could they do so ; but here the abundance of deer is so great that the lions are able to kill vast numbers, without making any great impression upon them."

"But I should not have thought," an officer said, "that a lion could run down a deer!"

"He cannot," Mr. Harvey said, "except for short distances. The South African lion is a lighter and more active beast than the northern lion, and can for the first hundred yards run with prodigious swiftness, taking long bounds like a cat. Stealing through the long grass, and keeping to leeward of the herd, he will crawl up to within a short distance unperceived, and then with half a dozen tremendous bounds he is among them before they have fairly time to get up their full speed. They hunt too in regular packs; twenty or thirty of them will surround a herd, and, gradually lessening their circle, close upon their affrighted prey, who stand paralysed with fear until the lions are fairly among them.

"I was once surrounded by them, and had a very narrow escape of my life. I had left my waggons at a large native village, and had ridden—accompanied only by my native servant—some fifty miles across the country to another tribe, to see whether they had lately been visited by any traders, and whether they had goods to dispose of. I reached the kraal in the morning, and the palaver with the chief as usual wasted the best part of the day; it was nearly dark when I started, but I was accustomed to ride by the light of the stars, and had no fear of missing my way. I had been only two hours on the road, when the sky became overcast, and half an hour later a tremendous storm burst. Having now no index for directing my way I found that it was useless to proceed; the plain was open, but I knew that a good-sized river ran a short distance to the north, so I turned my horse's head in that direction, knowing that on a river-bank I was likely to meet with trees. Several times I missed my way in the driving rain, for the wind shifted frequently, and that was of course the only guide I had.

"At last, to my great satisfaction, I struck upon the river and kept along its bank until I came to a large clump of trees ; here we unsaddled our horses, picked out a comparatively dry spot under a big tree, which stood just at the edge of the river, wrapped ourselves in our rugs, and prepared to pass the night as comfortably as we could. The river was high, and my only fear was that it might overflow its banks and set us afloat before morning. However, we had not been there long before the rain ceased, the sky cleared, and the stars came out again ; but as the horses had done a long day's work on the previous day, I determined to remain where I was until morning. Having been in the saddle all the previous night, I slept heavily.

The wind was still blowing strongly, and I suppose that the noise in the trees, and the lapping of the water by the bank close by, prevented my hearing the stamping of the horses, which, under ordinary circumstances, would certainly have warned me of the approaching danger. Suddenly I awoke with a terrific uproar. I sprang to my feet, but was instantly knocked down, and a beast, I knew to be a lion, seized me by the left shoulder. My revolver was, as always, in my belt ; I drew it out, and fired into the brute's eye ; his jaw relaxed, and I knew the shot was fatal. A terrible din was going on all round ; there was light enough for me to see that both the horses had been pulled to the ground ; two lions were rending the body of my servant, and others were approaching with loud roars.

I sprang to my feet and climbed up into the tree, just as two more lions arrived upon the spot. My servant had not uttered a cry, and was, I have no doubt, struck dead at once. The horses ceased to struggle by the time I gained my tree. At least twenty lions gathered round, and growled and quarrelled over the carcases of the horses. When they had finished these, they walked round and round the tree, roaring horridly ; some of them reared themselves against the trunk, as if they would try to climb it, but the lion is not a tree-climber, and I had not much fear that they would make the attempt. I hoped that in the morning they would move off; but they had clearly no intention of doing so, for, as it became daylight, they retired a short distance and then either lay down or sat upon their haunches in a semicircle fifty yards distant, watching me.

" So the whole day passed; I had only the four shots left in my revolver, for my spare ammunition was in the holster of my saddle, and even had I had a dozen revolvers I could have done nothing against them. At night they again came up to the tree, and in hopes of frightening them off I descended to the lower branches, and fired my remaining shots at brutes rearing up against it. As I aimed in each case at the eye, and the muzzle of my pistol was within four feet of their heads, the shots were fatal ; but the only result was that the lions withdrew for a short distance, and renewed their guard round the tree.

"You will wonder perhaps why all this time I did not take to the water; but lions, although, like all the cat tribe, disliking water, will cross rivers by swimming, and they seemed so pertinacious that I feared they might follow me. Towards morning, however, I determined on risking it, and creeping out to the end of a branch which overhung the river I dropped in. The stream was running strong, and I kept under water, swimming down with it as hard as I possibly could. When I came up I glanced back at the tree I had quitted. The lions were gathered on the bank, roaring loudly and lashing their tails with every sign of excitement, looking at the water where they had seen me disappear. I have not the least doubt but that they would have jumped in after me, had I not dived. I took this in at a glance, and then went under again, and so continued diving until I was sure that I was beyond the sight of the lions; then I made for the bank as quickly as possible. The river swarmed with crocodiles, and had it not been for the muddiness of the water I should probably have been snapped up within a minute or two of entering it.

"It was with a feeling of deep thankfulness that I crawled out and lay down on a clump of reeds half a mile beyond the spot where the lions were looking for me. When the sun got high I felt sure that they would have dispersed as usual, and returned to their shelter for the day, and I therefore started on foot, and reached my camp late at night.

"The next day we got in motion, and when, three

days later, we arrived at the kraal from which we had started, I rode over to the tree and recovered my revolver and saddles. Not even a bone remained of the carcases of the horses, or of my native attendant."

"That was a very nasty adventure," the colonel said. "Is it a common thing, caravans being attacked by lions?"

"A very common thing," the trader replied; "indeed in certain parts of the country such attacks are constantly made, and the persistency with which the lions, in spite of the severe lessons they have received of the deadly effect of fire-arms, yet continue to attack caravans is a proof that they must often be greatly oppressed by hunger."

"Which do they seem to prefer," one of the officers asked, "human beings or cattle?"

"They kill fifty oxen to one human being; but this probably arises from the fact that in the lion-country the drivers always sleep round large fires in the centre of the cattle. I think that by preference the lions attack the horses, because these are more defenceless; the cattle sometimes make a good fight. I have seen them when loose forming a circle with their heads outside, showing such a formidable line of horns that the lions have not ventured to attack them. Once or twice I have seen single oxen when attacked by solitary lions, come out victors in the assault. As the lion walked round and round, the bullock continued to face him, and I have then often seen them receive the spring upon their horns, and hurl the lion wounded and half-stunned yards away. Once I saw both die together—the bullock with one of his horns driven into the lion's chest, while the latter fixed his teeth in the bullock's neck, and tore away with his claws at its side, until both fell dead together."

"It must be a grand country for sport," one of the officers said.

"It is that!" the trader replied. "I wonder sometimes that gentlemen in England, who spend great sums every year in deer-forests and grouse-moors, do not more often come out for a few months' shooting here. The voyage is a pleasant one, and although the journey up country to the interior of course takes some time, the trip would be a novel one, and every comfort could be carried in the waggons; while the sport, when the right country was reached, would be more abundant and varied than in any other part of the world. Lions may be met, deer of numerous kinds, giraffes, hippopotami, crocodiles, and many other animals, not to mention an occasional gallop after ostriches. The expenses, moreover, would not be greater than the rental and keep of a deer-forest."

"Yes, I am surprised myself that more sportsmen do not come out here. In odd times, too, they could get good fishing."

"Excellent," the trader replied; "some of the rivers literally swarm with fish."

"When I get back to England," the colonel said,

" I must advise some of my friends to try it. As you say, there are scores of men who spend their thousands a year on deer-forests, grouse-shooting, and horse-racing, and it would be a new sensation for them to come out for a few months' shooting in the interior of Africa. I must not tell them too much of the close shaves that you and your friends have had. A spice of danger adds to the enjoyment, but the adventures that you have gone through go somewhat beyond the point."

CHAPTER XVIII.

THE BOER INSURRECTION.

THE next morning the lads bade farewell to Mr.
Harvey and the three hunters, and then rode on with
the regiment. The day passed as quietly as the preceding ones had done.

On the 20th the column was marching along a road
commanded on both sides by rising ground. The
troops as usual were marching at ease ; one company
was ahead of the line of waggons, two companies
marched in straggling order by the side of the long
teams, and the fourth company formed the rear-
guard.

Suddenly, without the slightest warning, a flash of
fire burst from the edge of the rise at either side.
Numbers of the men fell, and a scene of the wildest
confusion ensued. Some of the young soldiers ran
for shelter underneath the waggons ; others hastily
loaded and fired in the direction of their unseen foes.

The colonel and officers strove to steady the men,
and to lead them up the slope to attack the Boers ; but
so deadly was the fire of the latter, and the men
fell in such numbers, that the colonel soon saw that
resistance was hopeless. Many of the officers were
killed or wounded by the first fire, and in five minutes
after the first shot was fired 120 men were killed or

wounded ; and as the rest could not be got together to charge up the slope under the deadly fire of the Boers, the colonel, who was himself wounded, surrendered with the survivors to the Boers. Two or three mounted officers only succeeded in getting through.

When the fire opened, Dick and Tom at once threw themselves off their horses, and, unslinging their rifles, opened fire. When they saw the bewilderment and confusion, and how fast the men were dropping under the fire of the Boers, Dick said to his friend,—

"It is all up, Tom ; it is simply a massacre. We will wait for a minute or two, and then mount and make a dash for it."

Their horses were both lying down beside them, for the lads had taught them to do this at the word of command, as it enabled them often, when out hunting, to conceal themselves in a slight depression from the sight of an approaching herd of deer. Thus they, as well as their masters, remained untouched by the storm of bullets. The Boers almost concealed from view, steadily picked off the men.

"It is of no use, Tom ; let us mount and make a bolt for it. They must surrender in a few minutes, or not a man will be left alive."

They gave the word to their horses, and these leaped to their feet, and, as was their habit in the chase, dashed off at full speed the instant their masters were in the saddle. Bending low on the necks of their horses, the lads rode at the top of their speed. Several bullets came very close to them, but keeping closely side by side, to lessen the mark they presented to the enemy, they dashed on untouched. Looking round, when they had proceeded some little distance, they saw that four Boers had mounted and were in hot pursuit. Their horses were good ones, in capital condition, and had done easy work for the last few days. The Boers also were well mounted, and for three or four miles the chase continued, the Dutch from time to time firing; but the lads were a good four hundred yards ahead, a distance beyond that at which the Boers are accustomed to shoot, or which their guns will carry with any accuracy.

"We must stop this," Dick said, as they breasted an ascent. "If they should happen to hit one of our horses, it would be all up with us. Dismount, Tom, as soon as you are over the rise."

As soon as they were out of sight of their pursuers, they reined up their horses and dismounted. They again made the animals lie down, and, throwing themselves behind them, rested their rifles upon them.

The Boers, they had noticed, were not all together —two of them being about fifty yards ahead of the others. At full speed the leading pursuers dashed for the rise; as they came fairly in view, they were but fifty yards distant. The lads and their horses were almost hidden in the long grass, and the Boers did not for a moment notice them. When they did, they instantly reined in their horses, but it was too late.

M 264

"THE TWO SHOTS RANG OUT TOGETHER, AND BOTH THE
BOERS FELL LIFELESS."

The lads had their rifles fixed upon them, the two shots rang out together, both the Boers fell lifeless from the saddle, and the Dutch horses dashed back along the track by which they had come.

The lads instantly reloaded; but they waited in vain for the coming of the other pursuers; these on seeing the horses galloping towards them after the shots had been fired had at once turned and rode off. After waiting for a little time to be sure that they were not going to be attacked, the friends mounted and rode on. They did not retrace their steps to see what had become of the other pursuers, as it was possible that these had imitated their own tactics, and were lying down by their horses, waiting to get a shot at them, should they ride back. They now continued their journey at an easy canter, and late in the evening entered the little town of Standerton.

Standerton presented a scene of unusual excitement; teams of waggons filled its streets, armed men moved about and talked excitedly, numbers of cattle and horses under the charge of Kaffirs occupied every spare place near the town—it was an exodus. The loyal Boers, who were at that time in an absolute majority throughout the colony, were many of them moving across the frontier, to escape the conflict which they saw approaching.

The more enlightened among these people had been fully conscious of the short-comings of their own government, prior to the annexation to England.

Short as had been the period that had elapsed since that event, the benefits which had accrued to the country had been immense. The value of land had risen fourfold; English traders had opened establishments in every village, and the Dutch obtained far higher prices than before for their produce, with a corresponding reduction in that of the articles which they had to purchase. Peaceable men were no longer harassed by being summoned to take part in commandos or levies for expeditions against the natives. The feeling of insecurity from the threatening attitude of the Zulus and other warlike neighbours was at an end, as was the danger of a general rising among the natives in the colony, who outnumbered the Boers by ten to one.

Thus the wiser heads among the Boers bitterly regretted the movement which had commenced for the renewed independence of the country. They did not believe that it would be successful, because they could not suppose that England, having, by the repeated assertions of its representatives that the annexation was final and absolute, induced thousands of Englishmen to purchase land, erect trading establishments, and embark their capital in the country, could ever desert and ruin them. They foresaw, moreover, that even should the rebellion be successful it would throw the country back a century, the rising trade would be nipped in the bud, the English colonists would leave the country, the price of land would again fall to a nominal sum, the old difficulties of raising taxes to carry on the government would recur, and restless spirits would again be carrying out lawless raids upon the natives, and involving them in difficulties and dangers.

Farther north the loyal portion of the Dutch remained quiet during the trouble; but around Standerton, Utrecht, and other places near the frontier large numbers of them crossed into Natal, with their wives and families, their cattle and horses, and there remained until the end of the war. The English settlers, almost to a man, abandoned their farms, and either retired into Natal or assembled in the towns and formed themselves with the traders there into corps for their defence. The manner in which throughout the war these little bodies uniformly succeeded in repulsing every attempt of the Boers to capture the towns showed how easily the latter could have been defeated, had the British government acted with energy when a sufficient force had been collected on the frontier, instead of losing heart and surrendering at discretion. It is not too much to say that, had the British government stood altogether aloof, the colony of Natal, with the English settlers and loyal Boers, could single-handed have put down the insurrection in the Transvaal.

The news which the lads brought to Standerton of the unprovoked attack upon, and massacre of, the 94th caused a wild feeling of excitement. A crowd rapidly gathered round the lads, and so great was the anxiety to hear what had taken place that Dick was obliged to mount on a waggon, and to relate the whole circumstances to the crowd.

Englishmen living at home in the happy conviction that their own is the greatest of nations can form little idea of the feelings of men in a colony like the Cape, where our rule is but half-consolidated, and where a Dutch population, equal in numbers, are sullenly hostile, or openly insolent. The love of the old flag and the pride of nationality are there very different feelings from the dull and languid sentiment at home; and the news of this bloody massacre, at a time when hostilities had not commenced on either side, and when no overt act of rebellion had taken place, caused every eye to flash, and the blood to run hotly in men's veins.

Those who had hitherto counselled that the English settlers should remain neutral in the contest were now as eager as the rest in their demands that the place should be defended. There was but one company of British troops in the town; but within an hour of the story of the massacre being known 150 men had put down their names to form a corps; officers were chosen, and these at once waited upon the captain in command of the troops, and placed themselves under his orders.

The next morning scores of men set to work throwing up a breastwork round the place, cutting holes in the walls and houses for musketry, and preparing to defend the little town to the last against any attack of the Boers.

The moment that he had heard from the lads of the disaster to the 94th, the officer in command despatched a horseman to carry the news at full speed to Sir G. Pomeroy Colley, who was advancing towards Newcastle with the troops from Natal.

The same night a messenger rode in, saying that the Boers had raised their flag at Pretoria, had killed several English there, and were preparing to attack the little British force encamped at a small distance from the town ; that at Potchefstroom they had also attacked the troops ; and that the insurrection was general.

The next morning the lads mounted and proceeded on their way, and reached home late that evening, to the immense delight of their parents.

The news of the rising created a fever of excitement throughout Natal. H.M.S. *Boadicea* landed a rocket-battery and a naval brigade, who at once marched up towards the front ; and Sir. G. P. Colley, who commanded the forces, hurried every available man towards Newcastle, as the Boers were advancing in force towards the frontier, and were preparing to invade Natal.

Every day brought fresh news from the Transvaai. The little towns where the British were centred, isolated and alone as they were in the midst of a hostile country, in every case prepared to defend themselves to the last; and at Potchefstroom, Wackerstroom, Standerton, Leydenberg, and other places the Boers, attempting to carry the towns were vigorously repulsed. The news that a large force of Boers was marching against Newcastle caused great excitement in that portion of Natal; here large numbers of Dutch were settled, and the colonists were consequently divided into hostile camps. Large numbers of British colonists sent in their names as ready to serve against the Boers; but the English military authorities unfortunately declined to avail themselves of their services, on the ground that they did not wish to involve the colonists in a struggle which was purely an imperial one. For, were they to do so, the Dutch throughout the colony and in the Orange Free State might also join in the struggle, and the whole of South Africa be involved in a civil war.

There was much in this view of the case; but had a strong corps of colonists been attached to the force of General Colley, it is pretty certain that it would have escaped the disaster which subsequently befell it; for, being for the most part excellent shots and accustomed to the chase, they would have met the Boers with their own tactics, and thus, as the English settlers in the garrisons in the Transvaal showed themselves far better fighters than their Dutch antagonists, so Natal, where large numbers of young colonists had served against the Zulus, Secoceni, Moirosi, and in other native troubles, could, if permitted, have furnished a contingent which would have entirely altered the complexion of the struggle.

Upon the very day after the return of their sons, Mr. Humphreys and his friend Jackson, furious at the two attacks which had been made by the Boers upon the parties accompanied by their sons, rode into Newcastle and inscribed their names in the list of those willing to serve against the enemy. They also offered their waggons and cattle to the authorities, to facilitate the advance of the British troops.

This offer was at once accepted, and it was arranged that on the 26th the carts still on the farm should go down to Pieter-Maritzburg, and Mr. Humphreys wrote a letter to Mr. Harvey, telling him that he was, upon his arrival, after clearing the waggons of the goods that he had brought down from the interior, to place them at once at the disposal of the authorities for the transport of military stores to Newcastle. Bill Harrison was to go down with the carts, and to be in charge of them and the waggons on their upward march.

Christmas was held with great festivity, to celebrate the return of the lads. Mr. and Mrs. Jackson and Tom, and four or five young settlers in neighbouring farms were invited by Mr. Humphreys to spend the day with him. At his request they came early, and after the service of the church had been read by him the day was spent in festivity. The young men rode races on their horses, shot at marks for prizes of useful articles, presented by Mr. Humphreys, and at five o'clock sat down to a Christmas dinner.

The holly, the mistletoe, and above all the roaring fire were absent, but the great kitchen was decked with boughs. The roast beef, plum-pudding, and mince-pies were equal to the best at home, and no pains were spared to recall home customs on the occasion.

At one o'clock there had been an equally good dinner given to the labourers and their families belonging to the farms of Mr. Humphreys and his guests, and in the evening all assembled in the great kitchen, and to the tunes of a violin, played by one of the young colonists, a merry dance was kept up for some hours. The next morning Harrison started with the remaining waggon and several carts for Pieter-Maritzburg, and the lads were supposed to resume regular work on the farms.

CHAPTER XIX.

THE GARRISONS IN THE TRANSVAAL

THE excitement of the time was, however, too great to permit the lads to settle down quietly, and every day they rode over to Newcastle to gather the latest news. The towns which held out in the Transvaal were Pretoria, Potchefstroom, Standerton, Wackerstroom, Leydenberg, Rustenberg, and Marabastadt. At Pretoria, the capital, Mr. Edgerton and Sergeant Bradley of the 94th Regiment, who escaped from the massacre, brought in the news, and on the following day the authorities proclaimed martial law. Colonel Bellairs, C.B., was commandant, and the military authorities at once decided that the town must be abandoned, as, with its gardens and scattered houses, the extent was too large to be defended. A military camp was therefore formed outside the town, and to this the whole of the loyal inhabitants moved out. The civilians consisted of 975 men, 676 women, 718 children, 1331 servants and natives,—total 3700. In addition to these were the British troops. All horses were at once taken for the volunteers, among whom most of the white residents were numbered. The effective fighting force was about 1000—made up of four companies of the 2nd battalion, 21st Fusiliers; three companies of the 94th; 140 mounted volunteers, known as the Pretoria Horse; 100 mounted volunteers, known as Norris's Horse, and the Pretoria Rifles, an infantry volunteer corps, 500 strong. For the reception of the women and children intrenchments were thrown up, connecting the jail and loretto convent, and the defence of this point was intrusted to six companies of the Pretoria Rifles, under Major Le Mesurier. The camp was distant about a third of a mile from the jail and convent, and the approaches were commanded by three little forts erected on eminences around.

Several skirmishes took place in the last fortnight in December, but the first sharp engagement occurred on the 6th of January. Colonel Gildea took out a force of twenty officers, 450 men, a gun, and fifteen waggons to bring in some forage and attack a Boer position at Pienness River, about twelve miles off. Norris's Horse scouted in front, and the Pretoria Pioneers were detached to cut off the retreat of the Boers. The Boers were easily turned out of their position. Their defence was feeble; but several English were killed, owing to the Boers treacherously hoisting a flag of truce, upon which the English skirmishers, who were creeping forward, stood up, thinking that the Boers surrendered; they then fired, and several of our men were killed or wounded. The Boers being largely reinforced came forward to the attack, but were smartly repulsed. Our loss was four men killed and one officer (Captain Sampson); fourteen men were wounded. On the 15th another force started to attack a Boer laager, but found the enemy in such strength that they retired without serious fighting.

On the 12th of February an ineffective attempt was made to take the Red Horse Kraal, seven miles from Pretoria, on the road towards Rustenberg. The force consisted of twenty-two officers and 533 men. The carabineers under Captain Sanctuary advanced and attacked a large stone building, 1000 yards from the kraal. They were received by a very heavy fire from the Boers, who advanced in such strength that Colonel Gildea thought it prudent to fall back. This movement, covered by the horse, was effected, the infantry taking no part in the fight. Captain Sanctuary and eight men were killed; Colonel Gildea and eight others severely wounded. No further sortie was made during the continuance of the war, but the Boers did not venture to attack the British position.

The town of Potchefstroom stood in the district most thickly inhabited by the Boers. On the 14th of December, when it was reported that a large number of Boers were approaching, Colonel Winsloe, who commanded, sent Captain Falls with twenty men of the 21st Fusiliers, twenty-six men of a corps commanded by Commandant Raaff, and sixteen civilian volunteers to hold the court-house. The jail was garrisoned by twenty fusiliers, and the fort and earthwork, of some thirty yards square, situated about 1000 yards from the court-house, was held by 140 men of the fusiliers and a detachment of artillerymen, with two 9-pounders, under Major Thornhill. The three posts were provisioned as well as circumstances permitted.

On the 15th 500 mounted Boers entered the town. On the 16th fighting began in earnest, and the firing was hot on both sides. A very heavy fire was kept up on the prison and court-house. Half an hour after it commenced Captain Falls was killed. For the next sixty hours the firing continued, night and day, and one of the little garrison was killed and nine wounded. During the night the Boers broke into a stable close to the court-house, and from a distance of eight yards a heavy fire was kept up. During this time Colonel Winsloe in the fort had given what aid he could to the garrison of the court-house by shelling the building from which the Dutch were firing upon it. On the evening of the 17th he signalled to the garrison to retire on the fort; but, being completely surrounded, they were unable to do this. On the morning of the 18th the Boers attempted to set fire to the thatch roof of the court-house; and as nothing in that case could have saved the garrison, Major Clarke and Commandant Raaff agreed to surrender on the terms that the lives of all those in the court-house should be spared. This was agreed to; but two loyal Boers, who had been captured at an outpost, were tried, condemned to death, and shot. On the 21st of December the garrison of the prison, falling short of provisions, evacuated it, and succeeded in gaining the fort without loss. The Boers occupied the post, but were driven out by the shell-fire from the fort. Mr. Nelson, the magistrate, was taken prisoner in the town by the Boers, and kept in close confinement. Three of his sons got into the fort, and took part in its defence. Two of them, on a dark night, on the 19th of February, got through the Boer lines, and carried despatches from Colonel Winsloc to Newcastle, arriving there on the 5th of March, after many perils, not the least of which was swimming the Vaal River when in full flood.

In the meantime the attack on the fort itself had been uninterrupted. The very first evening the watercourse from which the supply of water to the camp was taken was cut. A well had already been commenced and sunk to a depth of twenty feet, but no water had been obtained. Fortunately the water-barrels had been filled an hour or two before the supply was cut, but these only contained two quarts of water per man. The weather was terribly hot, and the work of the men in the intrenchments was very severe.

On the night of the 17th Lieutenant Lindsell, with some of the drivers of the Royal Artillery, acting as cavalry, and a company of the 21st, went out to fill the water-casks from a stream half a mile away from the camp, and fortunately succeeded in doing so, the Boers not being on the look-out in that direction. This gave a further supply of two quarts per man.

The work of sinking the well had been continued without intermission, and a depth of thirty-six feet had been attained, but still no water was met with. A reward of 5*l.* was offered to the first party who struck water, and the soldiers off duty commenced digging in several places. At last, to the intense relief of the garrison, a party of Royal Artillerymen found water at a depth of nine feet. The well soon filled, and yielded plenty of water during the remainder of the siege.

A desultory fire was kept up until the 1st of January, when, the Boers being strongly reinforced, 2000 men surrounded the fort at a distance of 500 yards, and opened a heavy fire upon it. They did not, however, venture to attack the little garrison. On the 5th they occupied the cemetery, 300 yards from the fort, but Lieutenant Lindsell with a party of volunteers went out by moonlight and drove them out. The Boers then commenced making trenches, gradually approaching the fort; but on the 22nd Lieutenant Dalrymple Hay went out, carried the position from which the Boers had been most troublesome, and captured four prisoners, some guns, ammunition, and trenching-tools. From that time, although the Boers continued to throw up trenches, they contented themselves with a desultory fire.

The siege continued for three months and five days; at the end of that time the whole of the provisions were exhausted. Fever, dysentery, and scurvy had broken out, and many of the garrison had died. Out of 213 men eighty-three had been killed, wounded, or taken prisoners. In fact an armistice between the armies had at that time been proclaimed, but Cronje, the Boer who commanded the attack, treacherously concealed the fact from the garrison. When only three days' quarter-rations remained the garrison surrendered the fort, on the condition that they should be allowed to march down to Natal.

Messengers had reached Cronje nine days before with news of the armistice, but although he was aware of this he continued the siege to the end, the firing during the last week being heavier than at any time during the siege,—on two days alone 150 round shot fell on the fort. The Boers were afterwards obliged to allow that the surrender of the fort had been obtained by treachery, and to agree to the garrison being reinstated.

Standerton is the first town of any size on the main road from Natal to Pretoria, and is situated on the north bank of the Vaal River. On the outbreak of hostilities two companies of the 94th and one of the 8:th marched from Wackerstroom to this town, and Major Montague of the 94th Regiment arrived from Natal to take the command. The total strength of the garrison consisted of about 350 soldiers and seventy civilians. The Landdrost, J. C. Krogh, remained loyal and assisted in the defence, three forts were erected on eminences round the town, two outworks and many breastworks and rifle-pits were dug, houses interfering with the line of fire were pulled down, and other buildings in suitable positions were barricaded and loop-holed.

The centre point of defence was a building known as Fort Alice, 800 yards from the town, and a military camp was formed on a height one mile and a quarter from this point. Preparations were made to blow up some of the buildings, should the Boers carry the town, mines being dug and laid to the fort. A good store of provisions was collected.

On the 29th a scout on a hill signalled a large number of Boers were approaching Erasmus Farm, three miles distant from Standerton. Captain Cassell, with sixteen mounted volunteers, went out to reconnoitre. Two or three scouts were thrown out, and these arrived within 600 yards of the farm ; suddenly a number of Boers made their appearance, and Mr. G. B. Hall, one of the mounted volunteers, gallantly tried to cross their line to warn his comrades of the coming danger. Galloping in front of the Boers, his horse was shot under him; taking shelter behind it, he opened fire on the enemy, and so attracted the attention of his party. One man could not long resist 300, and Hall was soon killed. The alarm, however, had been given in time, and the mounted men fell back on the camp, exchanging shots with the enemy. The Boers now took up a position 600 yards from the camp, and kept up a heavy fire. Skirmishes occurred daily, and the enemy harassing the garrison from a height called Standerton Kop, Major Montague caused a dummy-gun, mounted on two waggon-wheels, to be placed in the intrenchments ; the sight of this frightened the Boers off Standerton Kop.

On the 7th of January a Swazi, named Infofa, who had greatly distinguished himself by his bravery in the Secoceni War, but was now undergoing a term of penal servitude for culpable homicide, performed an act of singular bravery. The Boers had during the night erected a small earthwork on the outside of the Vaal River; 400 yards nearer the town stood a house, and fearing that this might be occupied by the Dutch, it was determined to destroy it. Infofa with a party of Kaffirs volunteered for the duty; he crossed the river with his party, and the Kaffirs began to pull down the house. Infofa, however, took his gun, and marched boldly away to the Boer earthwork, 400 yards distant, to the astonishment of the lookers-on. It happened that at the moment no Boers were present in the works, and the man reached it without a shot being fired at him; inside he found some tools, and with these he deliberately set to work and levelled the breastwork; this accomplished, he returned to the party.

Until the end of the war the Boers were unable to make any impression upon Standerton, and whenever they approached too closely the garrison sallied out and drove them off.

At Leydenberg fifty men of the 94th, under Lieutenant Long, had been left, when the four companies under Colonel Anstruther had marched away. The people of the town, when the news of the rising arrived, offered to defend themselves with the troops against attacks; but Lieutenant Long declined to accept the offer. There were in the town 220 women and children, and only thirty-four white men who could be relied on; there were no defences and no water-supply, and as Lieutenant Long knew that three or four months must elapse before a relieving force could arrive, he decided that it would only cost the towns-people their lives and property were they to attempt to defend the place. He therefore advised them to remain neutral, while he with his fifty soldiers defended the fort. This they did, and the commandant of the Boer force, Piet Steyn, caused their property to be respected when he entered the town with his troops.

For three months Lieutenant Long defended the fort gallantly against all attacks. At one time the enemy set fire to the thatch roof of one of the buildings, but the soldiers succeeded in extinguishing it, although the Boers kept up a heavy fire; during the night the defenders stripped off the roofs of the remaining thatch buildings, and so prevented a renewal of this form of attack. The Boers cut off the water-supply, but the garrison sunk wells, and succeeded in reaching water in time. The casualties among the fifty men during the siege were three killed and nineteen wounded. At the end of the war a general order was published, conferring the highest praise upon Lieutenant Long and his little garrison, for the bravery and endurance which they had shown in maintaining for three months a close siege, and this without any hope of relief or succour. At the conclusion of the war Lieutenant Long was so disgusted at the humiliating terms of the treaty, and the surrender to the Boers, that he resigned his commission in the army.

Marabadstadt, though called a village, consists of only seven or eight houses. Sixty men of the 94th, under Captain Brook, formed the garrison which was stationed there to keep order after the Secoceni War, as no less than 500,000 natives inhabit the surrounding district. Fortunately the races were being held at the time when the news of the massacre of the 94th arrived, and the English inhabitants of the neighbourhood, who were present, at once responded to the call of Captain Brook to aid in the defence, and thirty white men and fifty half-castes enrolled themselves as volunteers. The Boers attacked in considerable force, having with them two cannons; but the fort held out until the end of the war, the garrison making many sorties when the Boers brought up their guns too close. At Rustenberg and Wackerstroom a successful defence was also maintained throughout the war by the British and loyalists; but no incidents of importance marked the siege of those places.

CHAPTER XX.

LAING'S NECK.

On the 24th of January General Colley's little column, consisting of the 58th, a battalion of the 60th, a small naval brigade, 170 mounted infantry, and six guns, moved out from Newcastle; they took with them an amount of baggage-train altogether out of proportion to their force, as in addition to their own baggage and ammunition they were taking up a considerable amount of the latter for the use of the troops besieged in the various towns in the Transvaal.

Mr. Humphreys and Jackson rode over to Newcastle to see them start, and the lads sat chatting to them on their horses, as the column filed by.

"I don't like the look of things, father," Dick said, "and if you had seen the way the Boers polished off the 94th, I am sure you wouldn't like it either. If we are attacked by them, the troops would, for the most part, be wanted to guard this huge baggage-train, and I am sure, from what I have seen of the Boers, the only way to thrash them is to attack them quickly and suddenly. If you let them attack you, you are done for. Their shooting is ten times as good as that of the troops; they are accustomed, both in hunting and in their native wars, to depend each man on himself, and they would hang round a column like this, pick the men off at long distances, and fall upon them in hollows and bushes; while, whenever our fellows tried to take the offensive, they would mount their horses and ride away, only to return and renew the attack as soon as the troops fell back to the waggons. Besides, with such a train of waggons we can only crawl along, and the Boers will have time to fortify every position. I wonder, at any rate, that General Colley does not push forward in light marching-order and drive the Boers at once out of Natal, and cross the river into the Transvaal; then he would have a flat, open country before him, and could bring the waggons up afterwards."

"What you say seems right enough, Dick," his father answered; "but General Colley has the reputation of being an excellent officer."

"I have no doubt that he is an excellent officer, father; but he has had no experience whatever in the Boers' style of fighting; he knows that they have often been defeated by natives, and I fancy he does not value them highly enough. They cannot stand a quick, sudden attack, and that's how the natives sometimes defeat them, but at their own game of shooting from behind rocks I believe that they are more than a match for regular troops. However, we shall see. As I am not going as a combatant I shall be able to look on quietly, and fortunately the Boers are not like Zulus, and there is no fear of non-combatants and prisoners being massacred. If there were, I tell you fairly, father, that I would cry off, and let the waggons go without me, for I do believe that things will not turn out well."

" Well, I hope you are wrong, Dick. But you have seen so much fighting in this country, during the last two years, that your opinion is certainly worth something. However, there is one satisfaction, there are a number of troops now landing at Durban and on the march up ; so that if this little force does get a check, it will soon be retrieved. Now, good-bye, lad ; mind, if there is an attack on the waggons, take as little part in it as you can, and stick to the position of non-combatants. If they would have had us as volunteers, we would have done our best; but as they have declined to accept the offer of the colonists, let them fight it out their own way. If they get beaten and the Boers swarm into Natal, as in that case they certainly will do, the colonists will take the matter in hand by themselves, and if we don't send the Dutchmen packing back faster than they come, I am a Dutchman myself."

Had Sir George Colley pushed on rapidly with his column, he would have passed all the points at which the Boers could have taken up strong defensive positions, before they could gather in force to oppose him, as he had the choice of three or four different lines of advance, and until the one by which he would travel was known, the Boer army was forced to remain inactive, awaiting his disposition. As soon, however, as he had left Newcastle, and it was known by them that he had started along the line of road to the west of Newcastle, they moved their whole force to oppose him, and took post on a position known as Laing's Neck, at a spot where the road had to cross over a steep and difficult ridge. Here they set to work to throw up intrenchments, and the leisurely, and indeed dilatory, advance of the British gave them ample time for this. Although the distance from Newcastle to Laing's Neck was but twenty-five miles, and the column, unimpeded by baggage, could by a forced march have seized the position on the very day of their leaving Newcastle, and long before the Boers could have moved their army to reinforce the little body who occupied the position as corps of observation, no less than six days elapsed before Sir George Colley's force arrived before Laing's Neck.

This time was spent in frequent halts, in improving the roads, bridging the streams, and other similar operations, all useful enough in their way, but fatal to the success of a flying column, whose object was to strike a sudden blow at the enemy, and to secure the road and passes as far as the frontier, in order to facilitate the march of the main column of invasion, which was on its way up from the coast. Dick and Tom chafed under the long delays, and twice rode home and spent a day with their parents.

At last, however, the column was in front of the enemy's position. The Boers, who were some 3000 strong, held a strong position on the line of the crest of the ridge, with breastworks thrown up in front. The total force of Sir George Colley consisted of but 870 infantry, together with the mounted men and guns; and to attack such a position, with a chance of success, every man should have been sent against the intrenchments. General Colley, however, seems at the last moment to have been alarmed for the safety of his baggage, which was menaced by parties of Boers on his left flank. He therefore prepared to attack with only five companies of the 58th—that is, but little more than 250 men, keeping the whole of the rest of the infantry in reserve, but ordering the mounted infantry to assist in the attack—a service which, upon such ground, they were altogether unfitted to perform. The result of such an arrangement as this was inevitable. Tom and Dick could scarcely believe their eyes when they saw this handful of men advancing up the steep hill, at whose summit was a force more than ten times as numerous, and composed of some of the finest marksmen in the world. The six English guns opened fire to cover the advance, and the 58th went gallantly up the hill. As soon as they approached the crest, a tremendous fire of musketry was opened upon them by the Boers lying behind the intrenchments. The men were literally swept away by the fire. Gallantly led by their officers, they pressed forward until within a few yards of the breastworks; then the Boers leapt to their feet, sprang over the works, and fell upon them. Colonel Deane, Major Poole, Lieutenant Elwes, and Lieutenant

Bailey were killed, and no less than 180 of the little force were killed, wounded, or taken prisoners. Few even of the survivors would have escaped, had not the mounted infantry, who had ascended the spur at a point farther to the right, made a gallant charge along the crest of the hill and checked the pursuit. The main body of the British advanced a short distance to make a demonstration, and prevent the Boers from following up their success. The whole column then fell back four miles, to the ground which they had occupied the night before. The gallantry displayed by the 58th and mounted infantry was the sole redeeming feature in the discreditable affair of Laing's Neck, where defeat had been rendered almost certain by the previous hesitation and delays, and was ensured by the folly of sending a mere handful of men to attack such a position. As the British fell back, the Boers advanced, and at nightfall placed themselves on the road between the camp and Newcastle, entirely cutting the force off from its base, and threatening both them and the town of Newcastle.

Several days passed, the attitude of the Boers became more and more threatening, and General Colley determined at all hazards to open the way back to Newcastle. On the morning of the 8th of February he moved out with five companies of the 60th rifles, two field and two mountain guns, and a detachment of mounted infantry; Dick and Tom obtained leave to ride back with the mounted detachment. At a commanding post near the River Ingogo Sir George

Colley left two mountain-guns and a company of rifles as a garrison, and moved forward with the rest of the column. The River Ingogo runs at the bottom of a deep ravine. Crossing this the English force mounted to the top of the opposite crest, but they had gone but a short distance farther when they were attacked on all sides by the Boers. The troops were ordered at once to take shelter among the boulders and bushes, while the two guns from the top of the eminence opened fire with shell upon the enemy.

Dick and Tom sought shelter with the rest, making their horses lie down beside them, and were soon as hotly engaged as the Rifles around them in answering the heavy fire of the Boers. The fight began at twelve o'clock, and raged without intermission for six hours; sometimes the Boers attacked on one side of the position, sometimes upon another. The ground was broken and thickly strewn with boulders and bushes, and favoured by these the Boers crept up sometimes close to the position held by the English. So accurate was their shooting that none of the defenders could show his head above shelter for a moment, and it was as much as they could do to prevent the enemy from carrying the position at a rush. The 60th fought with the greatest coolness and steadiness, and, numerous as were the enemy, they could not muster up courage for the rush which would have assuredly overwhelmed the little party that they were attacking. The two English guns could render but small service, the men being shot down as fast as they stood up to load, and every officer, driver, gunner, and horse was killed or wounded within half an hour after the action commenced. So incessant indeed was the rain of balls that the guns after the action were spotted with bullet-marks so thickly that it would have been difficult to place the tip of the finger upon a place unstruck by a ball.

When darkness put a stop to the fight 160 men —more than two-thirds of the force—were killed or wounded. Among the former were Captain MacGregor of the staff, Captain Green of the Royal Artillery, and Lieutenants Green and O'Connell of the 60th; while Lieutenants Pixney, Parsons, Twistlewaite and Haworth, all of the 60th, were wounded. Had the Boers taken advantage of the cover of darkness to steal forward, they must have annihilated the little force; but they believed that they had them in their power, for the rain had fallen heavily, the Ingogo had risen, and was, they thought, unfordable. General Colley ascertained, however, that it was still possible to cross, and with the greatest silence the survivors moved off from their position, the storm helping to conceal the movement from the Boers. Very quietly they moved down to the stream, and with the greatest difficulty succeeded in crossing; then picking up on their way the company and guns which had been left on the eminence beyond, the column reached camp in safety.

In the meantime reinforcements had been pushing forward from the sea as fast as possible, and on the 17th the column under Sir Evelyn Wood arrived at Newcastle, to the great joy of its inhabitants. For days an attack by the Boers had been expected, intrenchments had been thrown up round the great convoy which had been collected to advance with the force, and all the inhabitants who could bear arms, and many settlers from the surrounding country, had come in to aid in the defence, should the Boers attack it.

The arrival of the relieving column ensured the safety of the town, and the Boers between Newcastle and General Colley's little camp at once fell back to their old position on Laing's Neck, leaving the road open. General Colley and his staff rode in from Prospect Hill, the name of the camp, and had a consultation with General Wood. The 92nd Regiment marched out and reinforced General Colley's column.

The Boers' position at Laing's Neck was commanded by a lofty and rugged mountain, called Majuba Hill, on its right, and the occupation of this hill by the British would render the position untenable. It would have been an admirable military movement to seize this hill when the whole force was collected at the camp in readiness to advance, as, with their flank turned and a force advancing for a direct attack, the Boers must at once have retreated, but General Colley most unfortunately desired to retrieve the two defeats he had suffered, by compelling the Boers to fall back, before the arrival on the scene of Sir Evelyn Wood with the main body. He believed, no doubt, and with reason, that Majuba Hill once captured would be impregnable against any attack which might be made against it.

Accordingly, on the night of the 26th, with twenty officers and 627 men drawn from the 58th, 60th, 92nd, and naval brigade, he started from the camp with the intention of seizing the hill. The night was a dark one, and the march across the unknown country difficult in the extreme. The intervening ground was cut up by steep valleys and rapid ascents, and for hours the troops struggled up and down these places, many of which would have been difficult to climb by daylight. At last, after immense labour, the force reached the foot of Majuba Hill, having taken six hours in accomplishing a distance which, as the crow flies, is little more than four miles. At a commanding point near the foot of the hill 200 men were left, to keep open the communication; the main body kept on until they reached the summit, just before daylight, the Boers being entirely in ignorance of the movement which had taken place. The position was of immense natural strength, as it was only at a few points that an ascent could be made. On the summit was a plateau, so that all the troops not actually engaged in repelling assaults could lie down perfectly secure from the fire from below. At sunrise the Boers could be seen moving about in their lines. An hour later a party of mounted vedettes were seen trotting

out towards the hill, which during the day they used
as a post of observation ; as they approached the outlying pickets fired upon them. As the sound of the
guns was heard by the Boers below, a scene of the
greatest confusion and excitement was observed from
the height to prevail. Swarms of men were seen rushing hither and thither ; some to their arms, some to
their horses, others to their waggons, to which the oxen
were at once harnessed, ready for a retreat in case of
necessity. Then a great portion of the Boers moved
forward towards the hill, with the evident intention of
attacking it.

At seven o'clock the enemy opened fire, and the
bullets whistled up thickly round the edge of the
plateau. The main body of the troops remained in the
centre of the plateau, out of fire, small bodies being
posted near the edge to answer the fire of the Boers
and prevent their approaching the accessible points.
For five hours the musketry duel continued. So far
its effect had been trifling, a few men only being
wounded. The position appeared perfectly safe.
The Boers were indeed between the garrison of the
hill and the camp, but the former had three days'
provisions with them, and could therefore hold out
until Sir Evelyn Wood arrived with the main body
for a direct attack upon the Boers' position.

Between twelve and one o'clock the Boers' fire
slackened, and the besieged force thought that their
assailants were drawing off; this, however, was not the
case. Under cover of the shrubs and rocks the Boers

were creeping quietly up, and at one o'clock a terrific fire suddenly broke out, and the enemy in great numbers rushed up the short intervening distance between themselves and the scanty line of defenders on the edge of the plateau ; these, seized by panic, at once fled, and the exulting Boers poured up on to the plateau and opened a destructive fire upon the troops.

The scene which ensued was one of the most discreditable in the annals of the British army. Although armed with breech-loaders, and fully as numerous as the assailants who had gained the crest of the hill, the resistance offered was feeble in the extreme; had the troops charged the Boers, the advantages of discipline and of their vastly superior weapons would have been irresistible, and they could have cleared the plateau as speedily as it had been occupied. The great majority, however, were seized with a wild panic, and, in spite of the efforts of the officers, thought of nothing but seeking safety in flight. A few stood and fired, but how few these were can be judged from the fact that only one Boer was killed, one severely wounded, and four slightly so ; while half the British force were killed, wounded, or taken prisoners, the remainder managing to escape down the sides of the hill, and to join the force left at its foot, or to hide in the bushes until night. Among the killed were General Colley, Captain the Hon. C. Maude, Surgeon-Major H. Cornish, Surgeon A. Landon, and Lieutenant Trower of the naval brigade ; eight officers were killed, and seven taken prisoners; eighty-six men were killed, 125 wounded, fifty-one taken prisoners, and two missing. The fight, such as it was, lasted five minutes. The force which had been left at the bottom of the hill, under Captain Robertson, was also attacked; but, being admirably led by that officer, fought its way back to the camp with but small loss, the guns there assisting to cover its retreat.

The boys had not accompanied the expedition, and from the camp had watched the line of smoke round the hill, and had joined in the laughter of the officers at the idea of the Boers attacking so tremendously strong a position. Intense was the astonishment in camp when a wreath of smoke suddenly rose from the summit, and when this cleared away, and all was quiet, and it became evident that the Boers had carried the position, it was difficult to say whether the feeling of dismay or humiliation most prevailed.

With the defeat of Majuba Hill the war in the Transvaal virtually terminated. When the news reached England, the government declared that the honour of the British flag should be vindicated, and great numbers of troops were sent out to Natal; these marched up the country, and were in readiness to assault the Boers' position, when the English government suddenly gave way, and granted to the Boers all that they demanded, the sole provision insisted upon being a purely nominal sovereignty on the part of the queen, and an equally nominal protection for the natives—a clause in the treaty which, from that time to this, no attempt whatever has been made to enforce. Not only were the natives practically abandoned to the mercy of the Boers, to be shot down or enslaved at their will, as in former times, but the English settlers, who had for months made such a noble defence in every town in the Transvaal, were abandoned, and the greater portion of them, ruined and plundered, have long since left the country where, relying upon the empty promises and vain guarantee of England, they had embarked their fortunes. A more disgraceful and humiliating chapter in English history than the war in the Transvaal, and the treaty which concluded it, is not to be found.

After the battle of Majuba Hill Dick and Tom returned to their farms, resolved to have nothing farther to do with the business; there they have remained steadily since that time. Mr. Humphreys' plantation of trees now covers a great extent of ground, and promises fully to answer his expectations of eventual profit. Those first planted are attaining large size, and the thinning brings in a considerable annual income. His waggons are fully employed in taking down fruit to Pieter-Maritzburg. In another ten years Mr. Humphreys expects that he will be a very wealthy man; he is thinking next year of paying a visit, with his wife and two sons, to England, where John will be left to finish his education and pass through college, with a view of eventually entering the Church. Dick is quite contented with his life; he has taken no farther part in trading expeditions into the interior, although the profit realized in the venture under Mr. Harvey was considerable, but there is plenty of work on the farm to occupy his time. A large number of natives are employed in planting operations, and since the first year Mr. Humphreys has raised all his own trees from seeds. The breeding of cattle and horses has been abandoned, only a small herd and a flock of sheep being kept for home requirements, as it is found that the ever-increasing plantation and the great orchards of fruit-trees are quite sufficient to occupy their attention.

Mr. Jackson too is prospering greatly; influenced by the example of his neighbour, he too has gone in for planting, although on a much smaller scale than Mr. Humphreys, his means being insufficient to carry out such extensive operations. Tom and Dick are as great friends as ever, and, when they can be spared, often go out together on a deer-hunting expedition. Tom is engaged to the daughter of a trader in Newcastle; Dick, laughing, says that he shall look out for a wife when he gets to England. The prospects would be altogether bright for the emigrants from Derbyshire, were it not for the trouble which the weakness of the British government, in sending back Cetewayo to Zululand, brought about, and from the increasingly bad feeling growing up between the Boers and the natives, owing to the constant aggressions of the latter, and their ill-treatment of the natives, in defiance of the agreements in the treaty with the British government. If the day should come when the natives at last rise and avenge upon the Boers the accumulated injuries of many years, neither Dick Humphreys nor Tom Jackson will be inclined to lift a hand to save the Boers from their well-merited fate. The example of the successful resistance offered by the Basutos to the whole power of the Cape government has had an immense effect among the native tribes of South Africa, and sooner or later the colonists there will have a very serious crisis to pass through. Dick hopes that this crisis will not occur in his time, for Mr. Humphreys intends in another fifteen years, if he live so long, when his first-planted trees will have gained maturity, to divide his great forest into lots, to sell off, and to return to his native land. Dick quite agrees in the plan, and hopes some day to be settled with an abundant competency in Old England.

THE END.

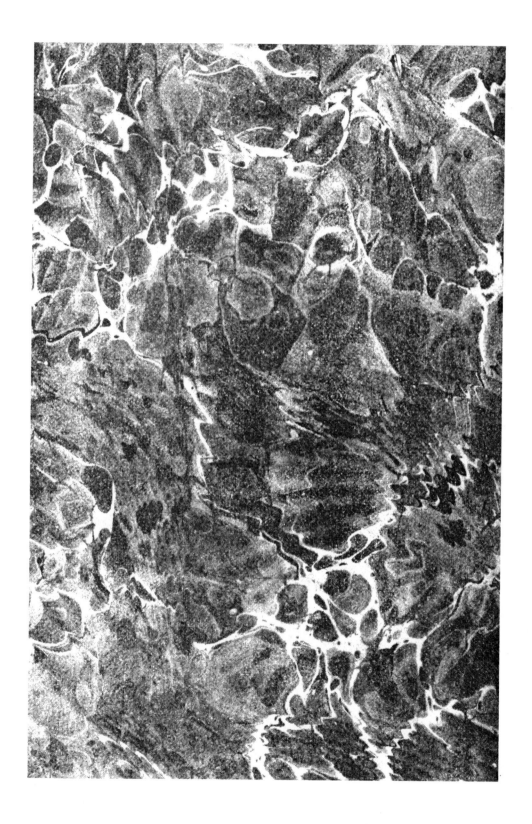

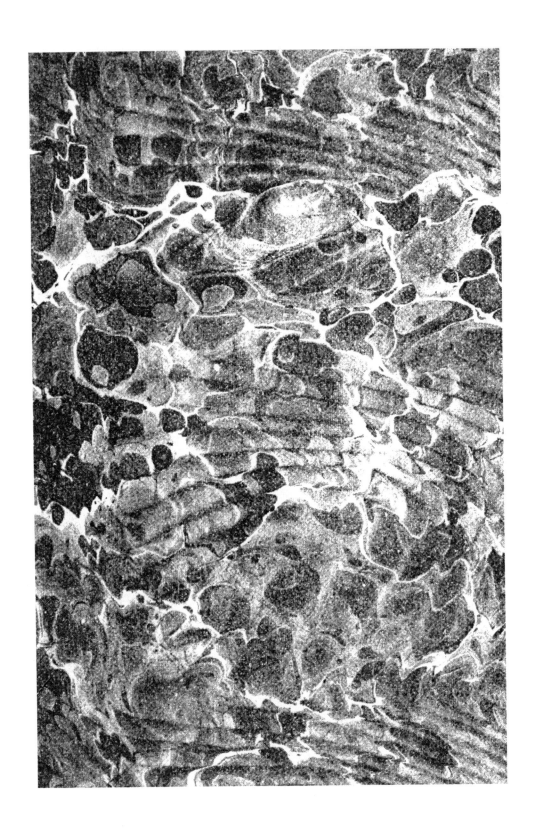